ASSESSMENT OF OLDER ADULTS WITH DIMINISHED CAPACITIES

2nd Edition

American Bar Association Commission on Law and Aging
American Psychological Association

AMERICAN BAR ASSOCIATION
Commission on Law and Aging

AMERICAN PSYCHOLOGICAL ASSOCIATION

American Bar Association Commission on Law and Aging

The mission of the American Bar Association (ABA) Commission on Law and Aging is to strengthen and secure the legal rights, dignity, autonomy, quality of life, and quality of care of elders. It carries out this mission through research, policy development, technical assistance, advocacy, education, and training. Learn more at www.americanbar.org/aging.

Collaboration with the American Psychological Association

This handbook is an update of the original collaborative work of the American Bar Association and American Psychological Association (APA). APA is the largest scientific and professional organization representing psychology in the United States and is the world's largest association of psychologists. The ABA/APA Assessment of Capacity in Older Adults Project Working Group convened in 2003 and jointly published three handbooks before concluding its work, *Assessment of Older Adults with Diminished Capacity: A Handbook for Psychologists* (2008), *Determination of Capacity of Older Adults in Guardianship Proceedings: A Handbook for Judges* (2006), and *Assessment of Older Adults with Diminished Capacity: A Handbook for Lawyers* (2005). The handbooks are available, cost-free, at: http://www.apa.org/pi/aging/programs/assessment/index.aspx and at www.americanbar.org/aging.

ISBN: 978-1-64105-916-9

THANK YOU

To the **Borchard Foundation Center on Law and Aging** for its financial support which made possible the preparation of this new edition

and

To the **ABA Section of Real Property, Trust and Estate Law** for its funding of the printing of the Handbook.

Contents

Preface

This handbook represents the second edition of the original collaborative effort of members of the American Bar Association (ABA) and the American Psychological Association (APA) which produced the original handbook in 2005. Since the original publication, the legal views of capacity have been heavily influenced by human rights trends, a growing awareness of the need for robust decision supports, growing concerns over abuse and exploitation of older persons, and more nuanced clinical tools for understanding and assessing the variations of capacity.

The resulting changes in this edition of the handbook include the inclusion of separate chapters on specific capacities and undue influence; a greater emphasis on the importance of supported decision-making strategies; greater attention to financial capacity red flags; and a greater emphasis on the fact that capacity is multidimensional and rarely an all or nothing proposition. This latter principle is even reflected in the slight change in the title which changes the original "Capacity" to "Capacities."

Even with the revisions, the handbook retains the strong base represented in the original handbook which was the first work product of the ABA/APA Assessment of Capacity in Older Adults Project Working Group, established in 2003. To produce this Second Edition, the ABA Commission on Law and Aging brought together an interdisciplinary team that included some of the original authors plus other experienced experts in law, psychology, geriatrics, and neurology.

Members of the writing, editing, and review team were:
Edwin M. Boyer, J.D
Jason Karlawish, M.D.
Daniel Marson, J.D., Ph.D.
Kyle S. Page, Ph.D.
Dari Pogach, J.D
Mary Joy Quinn, R.N., M.A.
Charles P. Sabatino, J.D., Project Director
Erica F. Wood, J.D
Jennifer A. Moye, Ph.D., Consultant

We dedicate this publication to the memory of Edward D. Spurgeon, former Executive Director of the Borchard Foundation and steadfast supporter, collaborator, advisor, and friend to the Commission.

We thank the **Borchard Foundation Center on Law and Aging** for its financial support which made possible the preparation of this new edition and the **ABA Section of Real Property, Trust and Estate Law** for its generous funding of the printing of the Handbook.

I. Importance of Attorney Assessment of Client Capacities

A. Capacity Judgments and Legal Practice

Although lawyers seldom receive formal training in capacity assessment, they make capacity judgments every time they interactively communicate with a client, whether they realize it or not. As a legal and ethical matter, capacity is presumed. It is only when a client presents signs that he or she is struggling with or unable to make an informed, independent choice, that capacity determination becomes a conscious mental process – one deliberately undertaken, haphazardly muddled through, or mistakenly ignored.

In the context of litigation, capacity may be the sole issue in controversy–such as in a guardianship action or a challenge to a will, trust, or donative transfer based on an allegation of legal incapacity. In this context, the lawyer's role is straightforward–to advocate fairly but zealously for the conclusion that represents the interests of the party he or she represents.

In non-adversarial situations, such as estate planning or the handling of specific transactions, issues of capacity are confronted more informally in the daily practice setting. In this setting, legal practitioners by necessity make implicit determinations of clients' capacity on at least two points.

First, the lawyer must determine whether a prospective client has sufficient legal capacity to enter into a contract for the lawyer's services. Failing this, representation cannot proceed.

Second, the lawyer must evaluate the client's legal capacity to carry out the specific legal transactions desired as part of the representation (e.g., making a will, buying real estate, executing a trust, making a gift, etc.).

Assessing a client's capacity may seem foreign and perhaps a bit alarming to the legal professional lacking training in capacity assessment or other aspects of mental health. The average practitioner may argue that lawyers do not and should not perform capacity assessments. Instead, lawyers should refer any cases of questionable capacity to mental health professionals for assessment.

The assertion is true as far as it goes–but it only goes so far. To decide whether a formal assessment is needed, the lawyer is *already exercising judgment* about the client's capacity on an informal or preliminary level. The exercise of judgment, even if it is merely the incipient awareness that "my client may need support to make a decision, or even with available support, lacks capacity," is itself an assessment.

It is better to have a sound conceptual foundation and consistent procedure for making this preliminary assessment than to rely solely on *ad hoc* conjecture or intuition.

Unavoidable capacity determinations:

1. **Does the client have the capacity to contract for my services?**
2. **Does the client have the capacity to understand and complete the legal transaction?**
3. **Are there supports and services that would address concerns about capacity and allow my client to contract for my services and/or complete the legal transaction?**

Lawyers need a conceptually sound and consistent process for answering these questions.

B. Increasing Prevalence of Capacity Questions

The incidence of cases in which capacity is an issue will increase substantially in the coming years because of the aging demographic bulge and because of the greater incidence of dementia that accompanies the aging process in the population as a whole. The label *dementia* implies no specific cause, nor does it represent an inevitable part of normal aging. However, the percentage of people with Alzheimer's dementia increases with age: 3 percent of people age 65-74, 17 percent of people age 75-84, and 32 percent of people age 85 and older have Alzheimer's dementia.[1]

A wide range of diseases affecting the brain cause dementia, some entirely reversible.[2] Alzheimer's disease is the most common cause, accounting for 60 percent to 70 percent of dementia cases.[3] New drug therapies are emerging to slow the progress of Alzheimer's, but it remains incurable and irreversible. For more information on dementia, see Appendix 4.

C. Decision Supports Can Address Concerns About Capacity

In 2005, we published a handbook for lawyers titled, "Assessment of Older Adults with Diminished Capacity." Our new title, "Assessment of Older Adults' Capacities," reflects a shift in legal and cultural approaches to capacity, including consideration of what supports would make it possible for an individual to make his or her own decisions.

An integral component of the lawyer's assessment of a client's capacity must include a review of existing supports and services that enhance decision-making, questioning what factors may be impeding the client's decision-making, and consideration of whether additional supports are available to foster the client's decision-making.

The shift in the approach to capacity from a static condition to a fluid state that can change based on available supports and services is evidenced by the growing recognition of supported decision-making. Supported decision-making is a decision-making model or series of strategies and principles that is gaining recognition as an alternative to substituted decision-making and guardianship.[4]

Supported decision-making can be defined as:

> a series of relationships, practices, arrangements, and agreements, of more or less formality and intensity, designed to assist an individual with a disability to make and communicate to others decisions about the individual's life.[5]

Supported decision-making is an important strategy within a much broader range of decision supports that can range from people supporters to technology, environmental aids, emotional supports, contractual agreements, and even court-supervised supports such as a limited guardianship using decision-support principles.[6]

D. Model Rule 1.14

The ABA Model Rules of Professional Conduct (MRPC), as revised in 2002, acknowledge the lawyers' assessment functions, and indeed, suggest a duty to make informal capacity judgments in certain cases. The revised rule attempted to give some guidance to lawyers faced with that task. Rule 1.14: *Clients with Diminished Capacity*, recognizes: (a) the goal of maintaining a normal client-lawyer relationship; (b) the discretion to take protective action in the face of diminished capacity; (c) the discretion to reveal confidential information to the extent necessary to protect the client's interests.

The trigger for taking protective action as directed by MRPC 1.14(b) is threefold, requiring:

MRPC 1.14
Client with Diminished Capacity

(a) When a client's capacity to make adequately considered decisions in connection with a representation is diminished, whether because of minority, mental impairment or for some other reason, the lawyer shall, as far as reasonably possible, maintain a normal client-lawyer relationship with the client.

(b) When the lawyer reasonably believes that the client has diminished capacity, is at risk of substantial physical, financial or other harm unless action is taken and cannot adequately act in the client's own interest, the lawyer may take reasonably necessary protective action, including consulting with individuals or entities that have the ability to take action to protect the client and, in appropriate cases, seeking the appointment of a guardian ad litem, conservator or guardian.

(c) Information relating to the representation of a client with diminished capacity is protected by Rule 1.6. When taking protective action pursuant to paragraph (b), the lawyer is impliedly authorized under Rule 1.6(a) to reveal information about the client, but only to the extent reasonably necessary to protect the client's interests.

the existence of diminished capacity; a risk of substantial harm; and an inability to act adequately in one's own interest. Lawyers are familiar with assessing risk and identifying what is in one's interest, but usually they are neither familiar with nor trained in evaluating diminished capacity. Even though taking protective action is permissive ("may") and not mandatory, inaction due to uncertainty puts the lawyer uncomfortably between an ethical rock and a hard place.

The drafting of Rule 1.14 predates much of the growing body of literature on and documentation of decision supports as described in Section C. Still, Comment 6 provides a strong foundation for lawyers to take the next step and incorporate decision supports into their assessments of clients' capacity:

> In determining the extent of the client's capacities, the lawyer should consider and balance such factors as: the client's ability to articulate reasoning leading to a decision; variability of state of mind and ability to appreciate consequences of a decision; the substantive fairness of a decision; and the consistency of a decision with the known long-term commitments and values of the client.[7]

While the Rule does not define capacity, Comment 6 recognizes that a client's capacity can change; it prioritizes the client's ability to articulate his or her reasoning over the lawyer's concerns that the client's decision is not in his or her best interests, and it considers the person's decision in the context of his or her previous commitments and values.

These factors blend quite naturally with the normal client interview and the counseling conversation. Yet the factors appear in the Comment without any conceptual, clinical, or practical explanation.[8]

Lawyers could naturally extend the guidance in Comment 6 to incorporate supports and services. For example, a computer device may facilitate the "client's ability to articulate reasoning." Or an attorney who has concerns about a client's "variability of state of mind and ability to appreciate consequences of a decision" may ask the client if she or he has a trusted supporter who can assist with making a decision.

See Chapter IV for more guidance on identifying decision supports for clients.

Comment 6 to Rule 1.14

In determining the extent of the client's diminished capacity, the lawyer should consider and balance such factors as:

- **The client's ability to articulate reasoning leading to a decision;**
- **Variability of state of mind**
- **Ability to appreciate consequences of a decision;**
- **The substantive fairness of a decision (will someone be harmed);**
- **The consistency of a decision with the known long-term commitments and values of the client.**

In appropriate circumstances, the lawyer may seek guidance from an appropriate diagnostician.

E. Legal Malpractice

Legal malpractice is another risk factor that points to the need for a more deliberate attention to capacity issues. The failure to assess a client's capacity has been asserted as grounds for legal malpractice by would-be beneficiaries of a client's largess. For example, a disinherited child may allege in a will contest that a lawyer did not exercise proper care in that he or she failed to determine the testator's capacity to execute a will.

To date, these cases are rarely successful, but the risk of being sued is real.[9] Traditionally, the courts have been reluctant to find lawyers liable for malpractice in these circumstances for two reasons: one, the lack of "privity of contract" between the lawyer and the disinherited third party (i.e., the lack of a legal relationship under which a duty arises);[10] and two, the fact that lawyers' conduct is judged by a standard of care established by the knowledge, skill, and ability ordinarily possessed and exercised by other members of the bar in similar circumstances.[11] Historically, most lawyers did not attempt to assess capacity, so consequently, the standard of practice was quite minimal.

However, the principle of privity has been eroded significantly over the years in case law, and standards of practice continue to evolve as the prevalence of incapacity rises and as a greater awareness of the need to address capacity issues has emerged. Legal malpractice for failure to address capacity questions in appropriate cases is a growing risk as the aging of the client pool and frequency of dementia rises.

This is not to say that every client should be referred out for clinical evaluation. Indeed, there are potentially serious negative consequences to such referrals, including increased costs and time delays and increased mental and emotional stress for the client. However, if there are any signs of diminished capacity, the lawyer is far better off consistently documenting the process of determining that the clint does or does not have capacity to engage in the transaction.

F. Attorney Assessment of Capacity

The purpose of this handbook is to fill in the conceptual background and to offer systematic steps in making assessments of capacity. The process does not plunge lawyers into the task of clinical assessment. Indeed, these guidelines recommend against conducting clinical cognitive screenings such as the Mini-Mental Status Exam (MMSE), unless one is professionally trained in such testing. Clinical screening tests such as the MMSE are often given too much weight. They do not in themselves provide sufficient evaluation of capacity.

This handbook recommends instead a systematic role for lawyers in capacity screening at three levels. The first level is that of "preliminary screening" of capacities, the goal of which is merely to identify capacity "red flags" and form initial impressions of a client's capacity status.

The process leads in most cases to one of four general conclusions:

1. There is <u>no or very minimal</u> evidence of diminished capacity; representation can proceed.
2. There are some <u>mild capacity concerns</u>, but they are not substantial; representation can proceed with or without decision supports to assist the client. An associated note to the file will be helpful in such cases.
3. Capacity concerns are <u>more than mild or substantial even with decision supports, or support is not available,</u> and professional consultation or formal assessment may be merited. Clear documentation of concerns and actions contemplated or taken will be important here.
4. Capacity to proceed with the requested representation is <u>lacking, even with decision supports, or support is not available</u>. The representation cannot proceed, and alternative legal approaches must be taken (for example, working with family members).

The second level of involvement, if needed, involves the use of professional consultation or referral for formal assessment. Such consultation or referral is best accomplished after the lawyer has fine-tuned his or her questions (see Chapter VIII).

The third level of involvement comes after consultation or referral and requires making the final legal judgment that the level of capacity is either sufficient or insufficient to proceed with representation as requested. Regardless of whether a clinical assessment is utilized, the final responsibility rests on the shoulders of the attorney to decide whether representation can proceed as requested or with appropriate accommodations to support the client's decision-making, or whether in appropriate cases, protective action under MRPC Rule 1.14(b) is merited.

The lawyer's assessment of capacity is a "legal" assessment. It involves:

1. **An initial assessment component and, *if necessary,***
2. **Use of a clinical consultation or formal evaluation by a clinician, and,**
3. **A final legal judgment about capacity by the lawyer.**

II. Legal Standards for Assessment of Capacities and Supports

This chapter describes legal frameworks for evaluating client capacities. Read in tandem with the next chapter on the clinical models of capacity, the explanation highlights the similarities and contrasts between the legal and clinical approaches.

The concept of capacity has been subject to rapidly evolving legal and cultural perceptions of capacity, including consideration of decisional supports and supported decision-making, emphasis on limited guardianship, and maximizing client self-determination. This paradigm shift in attitudes towards capacity should inform all approaches lawyers take in assessing client capacity.

Lawyers should use four models, sometimes individually and at times together, for assessment of client capacities. Taken together, these four models constitute the civil law's perspective on assessment of adult capacities, as set out specifically in state statutes, case law, and ethical rules and opinions:

(1) Assessment of supports and supported decision-making – explained in this chapter.
(2) Standards of capacity for specific legal transactions – introduced in this chapter and explained more fully in Chapter V.
(3) Standards in state guardianship [12] laws – explained in this chapter, and
(4) Ethical guidelines in Rule 1.14 of the Model Rules of Professional Conduct concerning clients with diminished capacity – explained in Chapter I and incorporated into the "Lawyers Assessment Worksheet" in Chapter VII.

Lawyers should understand four essential facets of assessment of client capacities:

1. **Supports and supported decision-making**
2. **Standards for specific transactions**
3. **State guardianship law standards**
4. **Ethical guidelines concerning clients with diminished capacity**

A. Assessment of Supports and Supported Decision-Making

The shift in attitudes towards capacity is evidenced by the growing recognition of the concept of supported decision-making – a decision-making model or series of strategies and principles that has gained recognition as an alternative to guardianship. As noted in the previous chapter, supported decision-making can be defined as:

> a series of relationships, practices, arrangements and agreements, of more or less formality and intensity, designed to assist an individual with a disability to make and communicate to others decisions about the individual's life.[13]

Identifying supports and services that enhance decision making can and should inform a lawyer's assessment of capacity. The lawyer's assessment should include examination of factors that may be impeding the client's decision-making, and consideration of whether additional supports and services could strengthen decisional abilities. Supports and service could include individuals acting as supporters, as well as technological, communication, and social services supports (see Chapter IV).

A growing number of states have enacted laws recognizing supported decision-making agreements. [14] A "supported decision-making agreement" documents an arrangement in which an adult chooses one or more trusted individuals – "supporters" – to assist with the steps of decision-making, including gathering and understanding information, reviewing available options, and communicating a decision. Supported decision-making agreements represent one important tool in a range of decision-supports that may include:

- Informal support systems such as personal relationships, community settings, religious communities, cultural groups and traditions, and a myriad of other supports systems.
- Direct personal supports from one or more friends, family members or other individuals,

Supported Decision-Making

- **Encompasses a series of relationships, practices, arrangements and agreements,**
- **of more or less formality and intensity,**
- **designed to assist an individual with a disability to make and communicate to others decisions about the individual's life.**

including, communication, analytic, or emotional assistance.

- Technology supports (such as a smartphone app or interactive software developed to support particular decisions).
- Environmental supports (such as modifications to the environment to enhance seeing and hearing of information).
- Psychological supports (such as ensuring decisions are made in less stressful places or without time pressure).
- Financial supports (such as direct deposit, joint accounts, or trusted person designations).
- Contractual supports (such as supported decision-making agreements or creation of a power of attorney or trust).
- Court supervised supports (such as the use of guardianship or conservatorship with decision support principles, or a protective arrangement for a single decision or action).[15]

Supported decision-making and other mechanisms for enhancing decision-making are increasingly appearing in statute and case law. Most state guardianship statutes require the consideration of less restrictive options, [16] and some include supported decision making or other supports and services, prior to the appointment of a guardian.[17]

In 2017, the *Uniform Law Commission enacted the Uniform Guardianship, Conservatorship, and other Protective Arrangements Act* (UGCOPAA), a model guardianship law that highlights supports and supported decision-making. The Act provides that a court may not appoint a guardian without examining the availability of "appropriate supportive services, technological assistance, or supported decision making."[18] Increasingly, judges are terminating guardianships when presented with evidence of available supports and services.[19]

Supported decision-making as an alternative to guardianship, and as a means for individuals with disabilities to exercise their right to legal capacity, is also recognized in international human rights law. In 2006 the United Nations adopted the *Convention on the Rights of Persons with Disabilities* (CRPD) recognizing access to the appropriate supports and services for people with disabilities to exercise their legal capacity as a human right.[20] While the United States has not joined close to 200 other nations in ratifying the convention, the CRPD plays a prominent role in the domestic discussion of supporting decision-making.[21]

B. Standards of Capacity for Specific Legal Transactions

While taking supports and services into consideration, a lawyer must be familiar with state-based standards of capacity for specific legal transactions. As detailed in Chapter V, lawyers work in the context of defined legal "transactions" or tasks such as making a will, executing an advance directive, entering into a contract, making a gift, voting, consenting to health care, or driving a car.

The law generally presumes that adults possess the capacity to undertake any legal tasks, but this presumption can be overcome in two instances: (1) the person is adjudicated as "incapacitated" in the context of a guardianship or conservatorship decision; or (2) a party challenging capacity in a particular context puts forth sufficient evidence to meet a requisite burden of proof. The definition of "diminished capacity" in everyday legal practice depends largely on the particular transaction or decision at hand, as well as the jurisdiction in which one is located.

Thus, in statutory and case law, legal capacity has multiple definitions. These definitions usually rely on the person's understanding of the issues and of the consequences of actions. For instance, for testamentary capacity, the testator at the time of executing a will must have capacity to know the natural objects of his or her bounty, the nature and extent of his or her property, and be able to interrelate these elements sufficiently to make a disposition of property according to an orderly desire. In determining an individual's capacity to execute a contract, courts assess the party's ability to understand the nature and effect of the act and the business being transacted. Chapter V summarizes the law and suggests practices concerning a range of specific transactions and domains.

C. Diminished Capacity in State Guardianship Law

State guardianship laws rely on broader and more encompassing definitions of incapacity, a finding of which permits the state to override an individual's right to make decisions and to appoint someone (a guardian) to act as the person's surrogate decision-maker for some or all of the person's affairs. The criteria for a finding of incapacity differ among the states, but in all states the law starts with the presumption of capacity. The burden of proof is on the party bringing the petition to establish sufficient diminished capacity to justify the appointment of a guardian.

Early state guardianship laws focused on medical conditions such as "mental illness," "mental disability," or "schizophrenia" for a finding of incapacity. Over time, states sought to move from a purely medical model to a combination of four related tests of incapacity:[22]

- Medical condition – While guardianship reform discourages medical labels, many states continue to include some types of medical conditions or diagnoses -- such as mental illness, intellectual or developmental disability, alcoholism, drug abuse – as one prong of their incapacity test.
- Functional behavior – States have sought to focus less on medical conditions and more on how individuals function in society. They use "functional behavior tests" requiring a finding that the person's functioning could put him or her in harm. The person must be incapable of self-care, unable to meet essential needs, or unable to provide for personal needs and/or property management.
- Cognitive element – A third test focuses on the cognitive aspects of decision making. It targets the person's ability to "receive and evaluate information" and "make and communicate decisions." Some states still insert a subjective element by requiring "responsible decisions." A few states, however, specify that "poor judgment alone is not sufficient evidence" of incapacity.[23]
- Necessity resulting from the risk of harm – A fourth test is whether the person would be subject to harm without the protection of a guardian, and an assessment of the extent and nature of the risk. In other words, the appointment of a guardian must be "necessary." For example, if the person fails to meet one or more of the first three tests but resides in a safe environment with regular support, a guardian may not be required. This suggests concepts of "supported decision-making," as discussed above.

The 2017 *Uniform Guardianship, Conservatorship and Other Protective Arrangements Act* (UGCOPAA) does not include the terms "capacity," "incapacity," or "incapacitated person." Instead, it defines "the basis for appointment of a guardian for an adult" as requiring evidence that:

> "(A) the respondent lacks the ability to meet essential requirements for physical health, safety, or self-care because the respondent is unable to receive and evaluate information or make or communicate decisions, even with appropriate supportive services, technological assistance, or supported decision-making; and (B) the respondent's identified needs cannot be met by a protective arrangement instead of guardianship or other less restrictive alternative. . . "[24]

Thus, the Uniform Act includes both functional and cognitive elements, as well as an assessment of necessity (needs cannot be met by a less restrictive option), but no medical conditions are included as an element of the definition. This helps counter the historical misassumption that certain medical diagnoses equal incapacity. However, as a procedural matter, medical evaluation is still important to ascertain causal factors for one's diminished abilities. As indicated earlier, the Act also strongly highlights the focus on supports and supported decision-making.

In addition to defining the elements of diminished capacity, most state guardianship statutes have recognized that capacity is not an all or nothing phenomenon, and have enacted language preferring or at least allowing for "limited guardianship," in which the guardian is assigned duties and powers only in those areas for which the individual is unable to make decisions.[25] Thus, judges, as well as lawyers who draft proposed court orders, must understand and identify those specific areas in which the person can and cannot function, leaving as much authority with the individual as possible, and accounting for appropriate supports and services.[26]

Taken together, these legal models for assessing client capacities – assessment of supports and supported decision-making, standards of capacity for specific legal transactions, and standards in state guardianship laws – complement the model based on ethical guidelines for lawyers in Rule 1.14 of the *Model Rules of Professional Conduct* and its Commentary highlighted in Chapter I above.

State guardianship laws mix and match two or more of the following criteria in defining Incapacity:

1. **Disabling Condition (often long list)**
2. **Resulting in Functional Behavior Deficit (focusing on essential needs or endangerment)**
3. **Cognitive Functioning Deficit**
4. **Necessity for Court Intervention**
   - **Or least restrictive alternative**
   - **Or with supported decision-making**

III. Health Professionals and the Clinical Model of Capacity

Health professionals from diverse disciplines have researched and extended the conceptualization of capacities, offering ways to incorporate a clinical perspective into a legal determination. In this chapter, we address the importance of the clinical perspective and the general model used by health professionals.

A. When and Why?

Why Should Legal Professionals Consider the Clinical Perspective on Capacity?

In most situations, the lawyer will determine that the client has legal capacity and will proceed with the transaction without need for an assessment by a health professional. However, a legal professional may want a clinical perspective to aid in their own understanding and presentation of a case. These evaluations bring in additional information on the client's overall functioning, including behavior, cognition, and decision-making abilities as it relates to the legal transaction in question.

For example, an evaluation may help a legal professional learn more about a client's memory and reasoning abilities during a time when a client wishes to create a living will or change a trust. Health professionals can also provide useful information on how to account for client cognitive and functional declines, to promote supportive decision-making arrangements. Finally, clinical professionals are essential for helping attorneys and courts resolve retrospective issues of legal capacity. Attorneys and courts are usually ill-equipped at forming retrospective judgments on their own.

What Are the Role Differences in the Legal and Clinical Determination of Capacity?

Health and legal professionals have different roles in the determination of capacities. However, both serve complimentary functions in how each understands and carries out the evaluation of capacities. Health professionals have contributed to the legal conceptualization of capacities, just as legal professionals have influenced how health professionals conduct these evaluations. A health professional's evaluation is a clinical opinion about a client's ability to perform certain tasks or to make a decision. Clinical opinions by themselves do not dictate legal decisions about capacity either by courts and juries or lawyers, but they help lawyers better formulate their own arguments and conclusions for and against legal capacity using legal frameworks based on precedent.

Key Points

- **In most cases, it will not be necessary to consult with a clinician.**
- **Knowledge of clinical models of capacity can be useful.**
- **Many legal and clinical concepts of capacity are similar.**
- **There is consensus on clinical models of capacity.**

Moreover, clinicians can offer insightful information on current physical and cognitive functioning, values, preferences, behaviors, history, and clinical prognosis (when and how capacity might be restored). But ultimately, the lawyer or judge will decide on the client's legal capacity to engage in a certain transaction or be recognized as having or not having legal capacity.

Which Health Professionals Evaluate Capacity?

Historically, when lawyers sought clinical consultation, they consulted physicians (such as a psychiatrist, neurologist, or geriatrician), but the range of resources today also encompasses psychologists, especially neuro-psychologists and forensic psychologists. Health professionals themselves typically also consider and integrate information obtained from other health professionals, such as social workers, occupational, physical, and speech therapists, in assessing capacity.

When working with a health professional, it is important to ask about their experiences performing capacity evaluations. Many professions also have subspecialties in working with older adults and these individuals may be well-trained in addressing the complex legal, ethical, and clinical situations commonly found in later life.

When Should I Refer to a Health Professional?

Lawyers may be wondering when to involve a health professional. It is necessary to refer to a health professional in certain situations. Some of these include:

- when there is concern about a medical or behavioral issue that needs clarification or attention (i.e., a client's new "fogginess" or confusion may be delirium and require prompt attention);
- if a client with an established cognitive diagnosis seems to be getting worse and the legal professional wants a current understanding of their ability to understand information presented to them and to participate in planned transactions;
- potential or anticipated family disagreement about a client's capacity to create or change a will;
- when examining if specific medical or psychiatric conditions may be influencing a client's decisional abilities; and
- to assist in determining if a guardianship is necessary or if an existing guardianship is still necessary.

B. General Clinical Model of Capacity

What is the General Model of Capacity Used by Health Professionals?

Regardless of the specific capacity that is being evaluated, health professionals use a general model to guide their work. This model provides a comprehensive understanding of the client's level of functioning. A widely cited general model of capacity is known as "the Grisso model" which identifies key components of capacity as causal, functional, and interactive (Grisso, 2003). A comparison of legal and clinical models of capacity reveals many similarities. We describe these key components below and how a health professional may approach the assessment of each. Importantly, just as the law has transaction-specific models of legal capacities, health professionals also recognize "domain"-specific models of capacities. Models for these specific "domains" of capacity, such as the capacity to consent to medical care and the capacity to live independently, are presented in Chapter V.

(1) Causal Component

Definition of Causal Component

The causal component is the cause or reason for the reduced capacity or inability to make decisions. Health professionals may express this in terms of a diagnosis. Knowing this information can potentially inform the legal professional in understanding the likelihood of continued difficulty, improvement, and even treatments to remedy the cause.

Assessment of Causal Component

Health professionals have a variety of ways they can assess clients (e.g., labs, imaging, structured interviews, questionnaires). Information collected can be specific to cognitive functioning, psychiatric health, and physical health. Of course, a clinician may determine that there is no diagnosable illness and that the person's current decisions (even if they represent a change from past decisions) reflect an appropriate, considered choice that is consistent with the individual's culture, values, and preferences.

Relationship to Legal Standard

The causal component in the clinical model will be familiar to legal professionals as the disabling condition test found in guardianship law (see Chapter II). Information about the likely cause of not being able to make certain decisions is very important information for the attorney. Once the

Knowing the diagnosis helps answer:

- **What is causing the problem?**
- **Is it temporary or permanent?**
- **Will it get better or worse over time?**
- **Could it improve with treatment?**
- **What treatment could help?**
- **Is there no clinical impairment or illness?**

diagnosis is established, it usually indicates the prognosis and likely pattern of symptoms. The diagnosis may also suggest to the attorney why a given client is frequently changing his or her mind. An answer to the latter question is especially relevant to the Comment to Model Rule 1.14, which asks for consideration of the client's variability of state of mind.

For example, an individual comes into a lawyer's office to change a will but seems confused. Knowledge of the cause of the confusion could help guide the lawyer's actions. A diagnosis of delirium (a condition in which an individual has marked difficulties focusing, usually caused by a medical problem) indicates that confusion is likely temporary and should clear up with appropriate medical treatment. A diagnosis of depression could suggest that a change of mind may be due to feelings of hopelessness or distorted thinking that should also improve with appropriate treatment. Thus, information on the diagnosis not only names the cause of any impairment, but indicates whether the impairment is temporary or permanent, will get better, stay the same, or will improve with treatment.

(2) Functional Component – Cognition & Functional Abilities

Definition of Functional Component

The functional component considers how well the client is functioning, that is, what a client knows, believes, and can do that is relevant to the capacity in question. This is different than the causal component above, as a diagnosis alone does not necessarily tell a professional how well a client is doing or the extent to which a client has capacity. Typically, these functional abilities can be considered across two broad areas: cognition and behavior.

Assessment of Functional Component

Cognitive abilities (such as attention, language, and memory) are assessed by health professionals through clinical interviews and/or formal testing. Interpretation of results also accounts for other factors known to influence cognitive functioning, such as level of education, age, and medical disorders. In addition, a health professional assesses other functional abilities (such as ability to manage medications or finances) through reports of family members, direct observation, interviewing, and/or performance-based testing.

Many traditional clinical assessments end once the person's diagnosis and cognition are assessed (e.g., a typical neuropsychological or neurological assessment). But, when legal capacity is questioned, it is important to have specific, direct information about the client's ability to perform the type of capacity in question, be it making a will, making a medical decision, living at home, driving, or any other task. The behaviors needed to demonstrate capacity varies depending on the transaction. Specific cognitive and behavioral functions for different legal transactions and clinical capacities are reviewed in Chapter V. It is the information about cognitive and behavioral functioning *together* that explains the person's capacity for the legal transaction or clinical capacity in question.

Relationship to Legal Standard

Legal professionals will recognize the clinical model's functional component as consistent with legal conceptualizations. Specifically, the cognitive aspect of the functional component is found in guardianship law, particularly those based on the 1982 or 1997 *Uniform Guardianship and Protective Proceedings Act* (UGPPA), or the 2017 *Uniform Guardianship, Conservatorship, and Other Protective Arrangements Act* (UGCOPAA) which emphasize an individual's ability to "receive and evaluate or make or communicate decisions" (1997, 2017) or "sufficient understanding or

Comparison of Guardianship Standards and Clinical Models of Capacity

Legal Model		Clinical Model
Disabling Component	↔	**Causal Component**
Cognitive Functioning	↔	**Cognitive Functioning**
Behavioral Functioning	↔	**Behavioral Functioning**
Necessity Component (Risk of harm & Least restrictive Alternative?)	↔	**Interactive Component**

capacity to make or communicate decisions" (1982). Finally, the behavioral aspect of the functional component is often found in guardianship laws that describe the need to adequately manage one's person or property. These elements are also found in all types of transaction-specific legal standards that characterize the specific skills or abilities for the transaction at hand.

(3) Interactive Component

Definition of Interactive Component

The interactive component of the clinical model considers the personal, physical, psychosocial, and situational demands placed on the individual. This component also incorporates the resources available, risks of the specific situation, and the person's values and preferences.

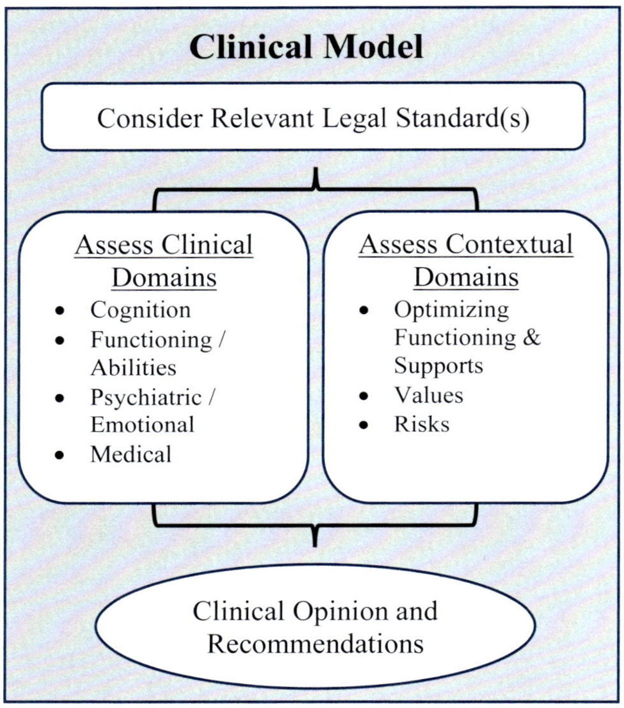

Assessment of Interactive Component

An assessment of the interactive component entails analyzing information about the client's level of functioning (i.e., abilities, information obtained from the functional component) and the client's environment (e.g., living situation, supports available). This component considers the extent to which the client's abilities and environment *match*. Consider the following situations. A client with an inability to remember new information after a few minutes would not "match" well to an environment that required him or her to manage complex financial affairs (here, the environment demands more than the client is able to do). Alternatively, a client with only mild cognitive decline due to aging may do well in a setting with consistent family involvement and automatic bill payments (here, the client's abilities match well due to the fewer demands placed on him or her alone, as other supports are in place to help). An evaluation will identify specific client strengths and where additional support is needed, quite important in the consideration of designing and advocating for supported decision-making arrangements.

Relationship to Legal Standard

Both legal and clinical models recognize the importance of understanding the interplay between the client's abilities and the demands of their environment. Legal concepts of capacity, particularly in statutory pre-conditions for guardianship, require a finding that guardianship is necessary and the least restrictive alternative given the person's circumstances.

A simple, practical way of understanding these differences between legal and clinical approaches to capacity is to recognizes that clinicians, in a variety of ways, parse and measure the operational cognitive, behavioral, emotional, and physical domains necessary to meet a relevant legal standard, which is often needed because legal standards tend to be defined in broad conceptual terms. Clinical findings and conclusions usually fall along a broad and multi-faceted continuum of capacity, while lawyers and courts are often looking for a yes or no answer. Lawyers still bear the final responsibility of judging whether to proceed or not with the legal transaction at issue. And, if the question of capacity is before a court in a guardianship proceeding, the court must come to the additional conclusion that guardianship is necessary because there are no less restrictive alternatives to guardianship.

IV. How to Identify and Address Barriers to Decision-Making, Including Implicit Biases, and Identify Supports and Services

Older clients face multiple barriers to decision-making and exercising their legal capacity. Some of these barriers are due to the realities of aging, including dementia, cognitive decline and hearing loss. Other challenges arise from external factors, such as the loss of a spouse or member of a support network. Some challenges have nothing to do with the client's cognitive health or circumstances, but rather stem from ageist attitudes about the ability of older clients to continue to make their own decisions.

Attorneys must carefully examine their initial concerns about an older client's decision-making capacity. Upon encountering an older client who appears to have memory loss or is nonresponsive to the attorney's questions, the attorney may conclude the client requires a surrogate decision-maker rather than considering what supports and services might address the issue. Furthermore, the attorney may not consider whether his or her implicit biases have led to an unfair or incorrect conclusion.

Recognizing biases, exercising cultural competence, and facilitating the client's decision-making autonomy can improve the attorney/client relationship. Lawyers may find they are more confident to move forward with representation when a client has the appropriate services and supports in place. Supports and services may also improve communication, enhancing the client/attorney relationship.

This chapter offers an introduction to the complex range of issues that present barriers to the decision-making for an older client. Every attorney should engage with these issues on an ongoing basis. This chapter includes references to widely recognized and publicly available resources that attorneys should consult for deeper insight into these issues and strategies to improve their own practice.

A. Recognize & Address Implicit Bias

Implicit bias refers to assumptions we unconsciously make about individuals based on traits or membership in a group. Like everyone else, lawyers and clients have implicit biases that inform their attorney/client relationships:

> When people meet, they form initial impressions that are shaped by visible characteristics such as sex, age, race, and bodily appearance. These traits tend to be associated with cultural stereotypes and with bias. And certain stereotypes are so deeply ingrained in our culture that people do not realize that they shape perceptions and behavior. Consequently, people may feel and exhibit bias toward people with darker skin, women, people with disabilities, or members of other groups implicitly. Indeed, implicit bias can take hold even for individuals who consciously reject stereotypes, racism, ethnocentrism, and so on.[27]

Recognizing one's implicit bias requires ongoing reflection and self-assessment. Consider the following first steps:

- Reflect on how cultural biases may affect your assessment of client capacity. Review and engage with the *Five Habits of Cross-Cultural Lawyering*, which include recognizing similarities and differences with the client, identifying alternative explanations for observed phenomena, reflecting on communication with the client, and addressing inevitable moments of cross-cultural blunders.[28]
- Take the widely used *Project Implicit* test, which has gathered data on thoughts and feelings outside of conscious awareness and control since 1998.[29]

Two ABA resources of note here are:

- ***Implicit Bias Videos and Toolkit for Judges, Prosecutors, and Public Defenders*. ABA Diversity and Inclusion Center.** ambar.org/diversity
- ***The PRACTICAL Tool: Steps in Supporting Decision-Making*. ABA Commission on Law and Aging (2016).** ambar.org/practicaltool

- Self-reflect on attitudes toward aging to ensure that "ageism" does not inadvertently influence your judgments about client capacity.[30]

B. Identify & Provide Decision Supports

Identify and facilitate decision-making supports and services for the client

Too often, we focus on what we perceive as the individual's weaknesses rather than focusing on how to support him or her enough to maintain independence. Client participation will engender client confidence in the lawyer/client relationship and the legal process. Useful guidance is provided in the ABA *PRACTICAL Tool*.[31]

The following suggestions are adapted from the *PRACTICAL Tool*:

- Identify areas where support is needed. For example, a client may have no trouble making healthcare decisions for him or herself but may struggle with financial matters.
- Ask if a temporary or reversible condition, such as a medical condition, sensory deficit, medication side effect or psychological condition is leading to concerns about capacity. If so, consider methods to address these concerns and/or schedule another client meeting.
- Ask the client about existing formally executed decision-supports as allowed by state statutes, including financial or health care power of attorney, advance directive or trusts.
- Discuss with the client whether he or she wishes to appoint a legal supporter or surrogate.
- Ask the client about family members, friends, caseworkers, or other community members who may provide support.

Concerns about supporters and risk of undue influence

Working with supports and services does not mean the attorney should ignore concerns about third parties. If an attorney has concerns about a so-called supporter's influence on a client, or believes the supporter has a conflict of interest, the attorney should discuss these concerns with the client.

Engender client trust and confidence

A client who is not comfortable in a meeting with an attorney may not communicate clearly and the attorney may not accurately assess the client's capacity to make a decision. Attorneys can take steps to build the trust of older clients, allowing them to be at their best during the interview process and bolstering their decision-making ability. Consider the following:

- Upon introduction, take time to "break the ice" and, if appropriate, make a few brief remarks about areas of common interest such as weather, sports, or mutual connections.
- Interview the client alone to ensure confidentiality and to build trust. However, consider the important role supporters can play. If the client is more at ease with a friend or family member in the room, consider including supporter for a portion of the interview. Be sure to talk *to* the client rather than past the client to others in the room.
- Stress the confidentiality of the attorney/client relationship. Some older adults may be fearful of losing control of their affairs if they divulge information. Assure the client that information will not be shared with others, including family members, without prior consent.
- Respond directly to the client's feelings and words, making the client feel respected and valued.
- Use encouragement and verbal reinforcement liberally.
- Conduct business over multiple sessions to increase familiarity and trust building.
- Make the office and counseling approach "elder friendly" and accessible to individuals with a range of disabilities. Under the *Americans with Disabilities Act* (ADA), law offices as "public accommodations" are required to make reasonable modifications to their policies, practices, and procedures to make services available to people with disabilities.[32]

Use Gradual Counseling

In 2006, this Handbook presented Linda F. Smith's seminal article "Elderlaw: Representing the Elderly Client and Addressing the Question of Competence," which describes a technique of *gradual counseling* that is useful in compensating for age-related differences in memory and problem-solving ability, and when there are questions about capacity.[33]

When this article was published in 1988, supported decision-making was not a recognized concept, but the article's methods for inquiring into and understanding the client's decision-making process provide an excellent foundation for assisting clients in thinking through their underlying concerns, goals and values, and choosing a consistent course of action. Steps include: Confirm or reconfirm the client's basic goal or problem to be solved.

- Confirm the client agrees with the lawyer's statement of the problem.
- Listen for important client values. Restate these values and confirm with the client. Recognize that the values of an older client may differ from those of the attorney. Throughout the counseling process the attorney should continue to reflect the feelings and thoughts that the client expresses to understand the client's values as fully as possible and confirm the client and lawyer have a common understanding of those values.
- Describe the best option for attaining the client's goal. Ask for the client's feeling about that option.
- Explain each relevant option and wait for the client's reaction. This will enable the attorney to see whether the client understands the information and how the client responds. It will also check for consistency of values. The attorney may need to "present fewer choices and only the most salient features for or against each alternative." This "weeding out" may allow a client of questionable capacity to reach a reasoned judgment.
- Give the client feedback that might be helpful. For example, if the client appears inconsistent in goals or decisions over time, pointing this out may help the client to remember and focus. If a client chooses a course that seems harmful, the attorney could express worry and concern, and get the client's reactions to this.
- Even when there is no clearly enunciated choice by the client, the lawyer still may be able to find capacity for the limited decision at hand from the client's reactions during the session.
- Above all, remember that it takes more time to support clients in this way, but lawyers should always be oriented toward maximizing the client's capacity to understand and make decisions.

C. Accommodate Hearing Loss, Vision Loss, and Cognitive Impairment

While not all older adults have hearing and vision loss, these deficits are common for a substantial proportion of Americans. Sensory problems, particularly in hearing, sometimes result in older individuals pretending that they know what is under discussion, becoming socially withdrawn, and in some instances, depressed.

And while not all older adults experience cognitive impairment, it is common that they may not grasp concepts as quickly as they used to, or that they need additional accommodations.

To Address Hearing Loss:

1. Minimize background noise.
2. Look at the client when speaking. Many individuals with hearing loss read lips to compensate for hearing loss.
3. Speak slowly and distinctly.
4. Do not over-articulate or shout as this can distort speech and facial gestures.
5. Use a lower pitch of voice because the ability to hear high frequency tones is the first and most severe impairment experienced by many older adults with compromised hearing.
6. Arrange seating to be conducive to conversation. Sit close to the client, face-to-face, at a table rather than on the far side of a desk.
7. Use written communication to compensate for problems in oral communication. Provide written summaries and follow-up material.

8. Have a digital personal sound and voice amplifier, such as a Pocketalker®, available in your office.

To Address Vision Loss:

1. Increase lighting.
2. Reduce the impact of glare from windows and lighting as older adults have increased sensitivity to glare. Have clients face away from a bright window.
3. Do not use glossy print materials which are particularly vulnerable to glare.
4. Format documents in large print (e.g., 14- or 16-point font) and double-spaced.
5. Give clients additional time to read documents.
6. Give the client adequate time to refocus his or her gaze when shifting between reading and viewing objects at a distance.
7. Be mindful of narrowing field of vision. A client may not be aware of your presence in the room until you are directly in front of him or her.
8. Have reading glasses and magnifying glasses available on conference tables.
9. Arrange furnishings so pathways are clear.

To Accommodate Cognitive Impairments:

1. Begin the interview with simple questions requiring brief responses to assess client understanding and optimal pace.
2. Conduct business at a slower pace.
3. Allow extra time for responses to questions, as "word-finding" can decline with age.
4. Break information into smaller, manageable segments.
5. Discuss one issue at a time.
6. Repeat, paraphrase, summarize, and check periodically for accuracy of communication and comprehension.
7. If information is not understood, incompletely understood, or misunderstood, provide corrected feedback and check again for comprehension.
8. Provide summary notes and information sheets to facilitate later recall. Include key points, decisions to be made, and documents to bring to next meeting.
9. Schedule appointments for times of the day when the client is at peak performance.
10. Provide time for rest and bathroom breaks.
11. Schedule multiple, shorter appointments rather than one lengthy. Multiple testing sessions can also assist in identifying the client's performance rhythms and cycles.
12. Whenever possible, conduct business in the client's residence. This often makes the client more relaxed, optimizes decision-making, and provides the attorney with clues about "real-world" functioning.

V. Specific Capacities

This chapter briefly tours several common actions or decisions about which capacity may come into question. These task-specific definitions of capacity are generally hammered out with greater or lesser clarity in litigation challenging the validity of some transaction, though some such a capacity to make a health care decision have been incorporated into state statute. While the discourse below accurately reflects the general approach to these specific capacities, the law is nevertheless abundant in variations, so it is important for lawyers to research the fine points of their state law.

A. Contractual Capacity

Relevant Legal Standard

Contractual capacity may be one of the most litigated specific capacity issues, primarily because the universe of human behavior is so heavily populated by contractual transactions. Yet, the legal standard for capacity to contract remains a general test of understanding, and thus, is cognitive in nature. In determining an individual's capacity to execute a contract, courts generally assess whether the person possesses sufficient mind to understand, in a reasonable manner, the nature, extent, character, and effect of the act or transaction in which the person is engaged.[34]

Capacity to contract is determined with respect to the particular contract in issue, and not with respect to the transaction of business in general.[35] Accordingly, if the act or business being transacted is complicated, a higher level of understanding may be needed to comprehend its nature and effect, in contrast to a simpler arrangement.

Purchasing a house with mortgage financing requires the buyer to make a series of decisions that will have long lasting consequences; buying a cup of coffee is a simple contract that does not require complex decision-making.

Functional/cognitive/other domains of capacity

Applying the legal standard requires inquiry into whether the person:

- Understands the general nature of *this* contract. (It is not necessary to understand every detail. Most of us do not understand, or even read, every detail of our phone contract or credit card contract).
- Understands the effect of the contract, i.e., generally what benefit they get and what obligations they assume.
- Has the level of understanding required for the degree of difficulty of the particular contract.
- Possesses the required level of understanding at the time the person signs the contract, not hours or days before or after the contract is made.
- Entered the contract voluntarily
- Can communicate the above, with or without assistance.

B. Capacity to Convey Real Property

To execute a deed, the grantor generally must be able to understand the nature of the act and to comprehend its consequences.[36] This is one kind of contract for which the same questions above should be asked to assess capacity.

C. Testamentary Capacity

Relevant Legal Standard

It is still common in documents to recite that the testator, or party to any other legal document, must be of "sound mind;" but by itself, that term provides no guidance. While the language varies slightly across states, the *Restatement of Property* provides a definition of the legal standard recognizable in any state:

> [T]he testator or donor must be capable of knowing and understanding in a general way the nature and extent of his or her property, the natural objects of his or her bounty, and the disposition that he or she is making of that property, and must also be capable of relating these elements to one another and forming an orderly desire regarding the disposition of the property.[37]

The lawyerly reference to "natural objects of one's bounty" refers not only to blood and adoptive family but also to others whom the testator considers family by affinity or who otherwise have a long-standing close relationship to the testator.

The test for testamentary capacity does not require that the person be capable of managing all affairs or making day-to-day business transactions. Nor must the testator have capacity consistently over time. Capacity is required at the time the will was executed. Thus, a testator may lack testamentary capacity before and/or after executing a will, but if it is made during a "lucid interval," the will remains valid. Finally, even a testator who generally possesses the elements of testamentary capacity may have that capacity negated by an "insane delusion" (i.e., irrational perceptions of particular persons or events") if the delusion materially affects the will.[38]

Functional/cognitive/other domains of capacity

Applying the legal standard requires inquiry into multiple cognitive functions specific to the testamentary process:

- Comprehension and judgment, which are required to understand what a will is, the extent of assets and the claims of beneficiaries;
- Long-term memory, which is probably the most essential memory task required for knowledge of assets and claimant/heirs;
- Immediate recall or registration, which is important because of its impact on cognitive performance in general; and
- Expressive and receptive language which are required to communicate with legal advisors and beneficiaries and to give instructions.[39]

D. Donative Capacity

The standard for capacity to make a gift would be the same as testamentary capacity except that it affects the donor's financial circumstances now and in the future, rather than after death. Thus, the *Restatement* provides:

> The donor must have the mental capacity necessary to make or revoke a will and must also be capable of understanding the effect that the gift may have on the future financial security of the donor and anyone who may be dependent on the donor.[40]

E. Capacity to Execute a Durable Power of Attorney

The standard of capacity for creating a power of attorney has traditionally been equated to the capacity to contract. However, some courts have also held that the standard is similar executing a will.[15]

F. Financial Capacity

Alleged loss of financial capacity is often the basis for judicial determinations of the need for conservatorship or guardianship of the property and estate of the alleged impaired individual.

Relevant Legal Standard

The 2017 *Uniform Guardianship, Conservatorship and Other Protective Arrangements Act*, Section 401 authorizes the appointment of a conservator only if the adult is unable to manage property or financial affairs because:

- the person has limited ability to receive and evaluate information or make or communicate decisions, even with the use of appropriate supportive services, technological assistance, or supported decision-making; or
- appointment is necessary to avoid harm to the adult or significant dissipation of the property of the adult; or obtain or provide funds or other property needed for the support, care, education, health, or welfare of the adult or of an individual entitled to the adult's support;

and

- the respondent's identified needs cannot be met by a protective arrangement instead of conservatorship or other less restrictive alternative.[41]

Functional/cognitive/other domains of capacity

Financial capacity is a medical-legal construct that can be defined as "the ability to manage money and financial assets in ways that meet a person's needs and which are consistent with his/her values and self-interest."[42] Financial capacity thus involves not only performance skills (e.g., counting coins/currency accurately, completing a check register, paying bills, purchasing stocks) but also judgment and decision-making skills that support a person's financial best interest and independence, and personal values that guide a person's financial choices and actions.[43]

Attorneys and courts often seek the assistance of mental health professionals such as psychologists and psychiatrists in evaluating the financial capacity of individuals subject to conservatorship and related legal proceedings. Clinicians bring a medical knowledge base, clinical interviewing and record review techniques, as well as functional, cognitive and personality testing in some cases, to the task of determining clinically whether an individual currently has financial capacity or had it at a prior point in time. Clinicians thus can offer valuable clinical evidence on financial capacity issues that can assist attorneys, judges, and juries in arriving at sound legal judgments of financial capacity and the possible need for conservatorship.

G. Capacity to Make Healthcare Decisions

Relevant legal standard

Over a century of court cases and legislation has enshrined the right of an adult to accept or refuse the health care she or he desires. In the early years of the legal and ethical transformation from a paternalism that included withholding information from patients to requiring disclosure of information, the ethic of informed consent was reluctantly, if not begrudgingly, taken up by medicine. Informed consent has now been fully integrated into the codes of medical professionalism. In the U.S., states have codified the legal standard for having capacity to consent. Across states, a core element is the ability to understand the nature and purpose of the proposed treatment or procedure, its potential benefits and risks, and the benefits and risks of the alternative approaches.

As stated in the *Uniform Health-Care Decisions Act,* capacity means:

> an individual's ability to understand the significant benefits, risks, and alternatives to proposed health care and to make and communicate a health-care decision.[44]

Some version of this definition has been incorporated into the advance directive laws of almost every state. An important feature of the definition is that it is decision-specific. Some health-care decisions are simple and some complex, so the individual may be able to make some decisions or consent to some treatments but not others.

Functional/cognitive/other domains of capacity

The emphasis on understanding means this standard is grounded in the clinician conveying facts to the patient and then verifying that the patient knows the meaning of this information using open ended questions such as "Can you tell me what the benefits of this surgery are?" This exercise of disclosure and comprehension relies on a patient having the ability to learn and encode information. Patients with deficits in memory, attention, language, and executive function are at risk therefore of having impaired capacity to consent to treatment.

Notably, the *Uniform Health-Care Decisions Act* does not include the ability to "appreciate" how the facts apply to one's situation or the individual ability to reason, but the appreciation standard can be found in many states' statutes or case law.

The clinical assessment of capacity for healthcare has generally been defined in terms of four dimensions or criteria: (a) Understanding, (b) Appreciation, (c) Reasoning, and (d) Expression of a Choice.[45] In addition, the clinical literature increasingly recognizes that accurate assessment of capacity to make a healthcare decision requires clinicians to consider the individual's strongly held values and beliefs, emotions, and life experience.[46]

As with other capacities, many individuals deemed to lack capacity to consent to treatment have not been provided with the appropriate supports and services to assist them in understanding and responding to novel and complex information. Simple mechanisms such as written summaries in lay language can assist a patient in learning and therefore processing medical information.

H. Capacity to Appoint a Healthcare Agent

Relevant Legal Standard

The capacity to execute a health care power of attorney is ill defined in most states. As with a financial power of attorney, courts would normally turn to the contractual capacity standard. [47] California and a few other states have adopted that view for ordinary powers of attorney in its probate statutes: "A natural person having the capacity to contract may execute a power of attorney." [48] However, as described in the discussion on capacity to contract, a standard based on understanding the nature and effect of a transaction provides only abstract guidance.

Since health care powers of attorney are creations of statute in every state and are applicable only to a narrow range of one's affairs (i.e., health care decisions), it makes sense to look at advance directive laws and cases to find articulation of a capacity standard. Unfortunately, few state advance directive statutes offer any guidance or statutory definition regarding the requisite mental capabilities and knowledge required to execute a health care power of attorney.

Two states, Utah and Vermont, do specify standards which, in differing language, prescribe components of understanding, appreciation of a relationship, and ability to communicate an intent to appoint an agent. Utah further makes a very important distinction, that an individual may lack the capacity to make a health care decision but retain the capacity to appoint a health care agent. Given the dearth of other guidance, these two states provide a useful model for practitioners, regardless of state.

Functional/cognitive/other domains of capacity

Reviewing these two state statutes, and the wider law, science, and ethics underlying the task of appointing a health care agent, Moyer *et. al* breaks down the cognitive elements necessary to appoint a health care agent into the following:

The individual must have the capacity to understand:

a. What it means to give authority to another for healthcare decisions
b. through a legal instrument
c. because of future (or present) inability to make treatment decisions

And to make a choice, which requires:

a. the ability to determine who would be an appropriate agent, and
b. the ability to express a consistent choice of an appropriate agent.[49]

The lawyer can best screen the client's capacity to execute a health care power of attorney and support the client's decisional ability by talking through the above elements one by one with the client, utilizing the counseling skills described in Chapter IV. Determining who may be an "appropriate" agent requires appreciation of relationship, history, and the agent's ability. Yet, in the end, having capacity to appoint a healthcare agent does not require that one be able to pick the best agent, but rather only one who is not frankly inappropriate.

For persons more vulnerable, the risk environment of their caregiving situation needs to be considered by the lawyer so that there is some level of confidence that the chosen agent will support the client's values, wishes, goals of care, and best interest.

I. Independent Living

Capacity to live independently denotes whether an individual can live at a residence of their choosing (such as in their home, an apartment, an assisted living facility, etc.). Questions about capacity to live independently frequently occur in geriatric care, especially considering how the cumulative effects of aging and illness can create challenges. Concerns about an older client's ability to care for themselves and manage their home environment often arise during periods of transition. For example, a medical team or family member may question whether an older adult can return home after a series of repeated falls at home, after a stroke, or progression of their neurocognitive disorder (i.e., dementia).

Relevant Legal Standard

There are no specific legal standards regarding an older adult's capacity to live independently in the community. However, legal standards are often found in state guardianship and conservatorship statutes. Additional legal standards may be found in statutes related to adult protection services and may consider psychiatric or physical health conditions or the client's functional abilities, such as whether they are dependent on others, unable to delegate authority, or unable to protect themselves.

Functional/cognitive/other domains of capacity

A clinical assessment may be beneficial when there is concern about whether an older client can remain in their current living environment. Clinicians consider relevant contextual factors, such as the physical environment of the residence, the client's physical and cognitive functioning, medical needs, financial management, and current supports/assistance received. In this sense, an evaluation of independent living capacity involves a range of skills and decisional abilities (i.e., can the client recognize and address needs and concerns). Emerging models for assessing capacity to live independently consider:

- Demonstration of the skills necessary for living at their desired level, to include activities of daily living (e.g., bathing, grooming, dressing) and instrumental activities of daily living (e.g., shopping, cooking, obtaining transportation, managing money, managing medications). If a person is unable to physically complete a task, can they direct someone else to assist them?
- Capacity to make decisions related to living independently. This entails considering the client's understanding of the basic requirements of maintaining independence at the level they desire (e.g., awareness of bills to pay, how to contact emergency services) and their current capabilities. Moreover, clinicians also evaluate an older adult's appreciation and reasoning abilities. These skills are important for anticipating and recognizing problems as they may arise in their environment, as well as problem solving and handling emergencies.

Older adults with reduced ability to live independently are at higher risk for self-neglect, elder abuse, and repeated hospitalizations. Clinicians, lawyers, and social service professionals can assist in identifying resources and assistance to support the older adult in a setting that balances risk, safety, and autonomy. Strategies are unique to each situation, but may include increased family visitation, automatic bill payments, or even relocation to a higher level of care where more support and monitoring can be provided (e.g., assisted living, nursing home).

J. Capacity to Marry

Although the institution of marriage is founded on the agreement between the parties, it is more than just a contract. "When formed, a relationship is created between the parties which they cannot change on their own. The rights and obligations depend not on the agreement, but upon the law. It is an institution of society, regulated and controlled by public authority.[50]

Relevant Legal Standard

The modern-day legal standards for determining capacity to marry are based upon this view and are grounded in the Common Law of England.[51] Under common law there was a legal presumption that a marriage was valid and getting married was easy.[52] Marriage was viewed as a simple contract, with a very low legal standard for capacity, requiring the capacity to understand the nature of the contract, and the duties and responsibilities which it creates.[53] As one English court put it:

> Capacity existed if the parties understood that the relationship was legally monogamous, interminable except for death or divorce, and that it involved mutual support and cohabitation.[54]

Today, states differ widely in marriage laws, but the majority, by case law, have adopted the above common law standard of capacity to marry.[55] The Common law standard is also reflected in *The Uniform Marriage and Divorce Act*.[56]

Functional/cognitive/other domains of capacity

Cognitive and functional behavior necessary to meet the standard established by the rule is, at a minimum, that the individual should know and be able to understand and communicate the nature of the marriage contract (who they are marrying, that it is consensual, the legal licensing and ceremonial components of how to get married, the permanency of the marriage except for death or divorce, exclusivity of the marriage, and how to terminate the marriage).[57]

The individual should also be able to articulate and communicate the duties and obligations which marriage creates (mutual obligation of mutual support and cohabitation, sharing of common domestic life and, enjoying each other's comfort and assistance).[58] With questioning directed at these components, the interview process can elicit the individual's explanation of why the individual is getting married, what makes a good marriage, and how that relates to the individual's situation.

The individual may be able to articulate the nature of the marriage contract and duties and responsibilities, but he or she needs to have the necessary skills and abilities to carry out the task. This would include determining if they can get the license, arranging the ceremony, and carrying out the duties and responsibilities of marriage.[59]

Getting married and carrying out the duties and responsibilities of marriage can be supported by someone who can assist in getting the license, arranging for the ceremony to legally finalize the marriage, and counseling and guidance on how best to carry out the duties and responsibilities of marriage.[60]

The attorney can be involved in this process by fully explaining the legal standards of marriage in their jurisdiction, and in assisting in identifying supportive resources in the community and appropriate support individuals.

K. Capacity to Mediate

Mediation is an informal process in which a trained neutral mediator helps parties find solutions to disputes. It can be used to address a broad range of conflicts involving older adults, including issues that might otherwise be litigated. Mediation can allow older adults a voice about preferences and choices in their lives.

Relevant Legal Standard

There is no clear legal standard defined in statute or case law. However, the *ADA Mediation Guidelines* name several factors to be considered by mediators in assessing a party's capacity: "The mediator should ascertain that a party understands the nature of the mediation process, who the parties are, the role of the mediator, the parties' relationship to the mediator, and the issues at hand. The mediator should determine whether the party can assess options and make and keep an agreement."[61]

However, some mediation experts have cautioned that overly strict criteria for mediation capacity could "raise the bar too high," as mediation is meant to be an inclusive and empowering process.[62] Moreover, mediators should consider the complexity of the conflict and whether legal rights are at stake. For example, an age discrimination dispute may call for a different level of understanding than a family or neighborhood conflict.

As with other capacities, mediators should ask whether the party needs accommodations and supports – for instance scheduling sessions at certain times of day, or in familiar surroundings, or using a series of short sessions. A supporter may accompany the person at a mediation – heightening capacity and helping to level the playing field. But the mediator must be alert to possible differences in values and perspectives between the supporter and the party and must ensure that the party is the key voice and decision-maker in fashioning any agreement.[63]

L. Capacity to Testify

Under Federal Rules of Evidence 601, every person is presumed competent to be a witness. The federal rules do not specify "mental qualifications;" lack of capacity is seldom sufficient to deny a witness the opportunity to testify.[64]

In civil actions, competency is determinable in accordance with State law (when specified).[65] An individual with diminished capacity in some areas of decision making may very well have the capacity to testify; adjudications of incapacity in other areas should not have bearing on the individual's capacity to testify.[66]

In a criminal trial, a jury determines the witness's credibility, but a judge determines the witness's competence to testify. In a criminal or civil trial, a judge should ask two questions when assessing a witness's capacity to testify: (1) whether the proposed witness can give an oath or affirmation to testify truthfully,[67] and (2) whether the witness is capable of giving an accurate account of what he or she has seen and heard.[68]

Judges have considerable discretion in determining whether evidence of the witness's disability is admissible to challenge the witness's credibility.

Other capacity questions also arise in criminal trials but are beyond the scope of this handbook.

M. Sexual Consent Capacity

Sexual consent capacity is a psycho-legal construct representing the ability to make one's own decisions about engaging in sexual and intimate behaviors with another consenting adult. As sexuality is an integral part of one's life across the span of adulthood, careful consideration of this capacity is necessary in order to promote the individual's rights, while also balancing the needs to protect individuals at risk of harm. The capacity to understand and consent to sexual activity is important in determining whether a crime has taken place.

Relevant Legal Standard

No uniform standard exists for a legal determination of capacity to consent to sexual activity among older adults with diminished cognitive abilities. All state statutes consider the ability to understand information related to the activity, but specifying what understanding is or the extent of information one needs to understand differs across jurisdictions.[69] Most states consider factors like those found in a clinical assessment (knowledge, decision-making abilities, and voluntariness), but can also be placed on a continuum of requirements to demonstrate this capacity. For example, some states may require additional consideration of awareness of the consequences of the sexual activity or even the morality of the act. [70]

Functional/cognitive/other domains of capacity

A clinical assessment may be beneficial when lawyers are concerned about a client's capacity to consent to sexual activity. While the clinical assessment of sexual consent capacity has not developed conceptually as much as seen in other areas of capacity (e.g., medical consent, financial capacity), a clinical model for assessment focuses on three components:[71]

- Knowledge of the sexual activity in question, potential consequences such as sexually transmitted diseases, and how to determine whether the partner consents to the activity,
- Decision-making abilities such as understanding and appreciating the behavior and expressing a choice about engagement based on consideration of relevant information and personal values, and
- Voluntariness of the decision to engage in the sexual activity and review of any potential concerns for physical or sexual abuse or undue influence.

Across these three components, clinicians consider several additional factors, such as current cognitive functioning (including strengths and areas of concern), physical health, emotional and mental health, as well as the older adult's values, perception of intimacy, and sexual and relationship history. As each situation is unique in terms of behavior, interpersonal factors, and abilities, a clinical view of sexual consent capacity also includes the client's awareness of safety, legality, and the level of risk involved (i.e., what is the risk of getting a sexually transmitted disease). Similar to a clinical approach to evaluating capacity to make medical decisions, an older adult may have capacity to make a decision about one type of sexual or intimate act, but not another.

Despite largely negative attitudes and beliefs about sexuality in later life, sexual interest and activity remains widespread among middle-aged and older adults. [72] Sexual activity decreases in later life, due to functional and physical changes, but remains important for sense of self and well-being. [73] Among older adults specifically, sexual intimacy may have a broader definition beyond intercourse (e.g., kissing, holding hands) to account for bodily changes. [74] As questions about capacity to consent to sexual activity arise, it is important to be mindful of ways we can support a client feeling loved and appreciated, even if that means exploring alternative ways to express these feelings.

VI. Screening for Undue Influence

The goal of this chapter is to review salient features of undue influence and to provide a practical screening tool that, while developed to parallel the law of California, may be helpful to lawyers and other disciplines as a practical screening tool under the laws of other states.

Undue influence is a separate issue from capacity. Under the right circumstances, any adult of any age can be unduly influenced, including individuals whose legal capacity is not in question in any way. It is also true, however, that it can be easier to unduly influence someone who has diminished capacity or who is vulnerable under stressful circumstances, such as recent bereavement, a major life transition, illness, isolation, substance abuse, or imminent death.[75] Thus, diminished capacity is a significant risk factor for undue influence.

The Estate of Olson (1912) affirms that an individual need not have diminished capacity in any area to experience undue influence:

> Soundness of mind and body does not imply immunity from undue influence. It may require greater ingenuity to unduly influence a person of sound mind and body, and more evidence may be required to show that such a person was overcome than in the case of one weak of body and mind. But history and experience teach that minds of strong men and women have been overborne, and they have been by a master mind persuadec to consent to what in their sober and normal moments, and free from undue influence, they would not have done.[76]

A. What is Undue Influence?

Undue influence is a process that occurs when one person (influencer) uses his or her role and power to exploit the trust, dependency, and fears of another person (victim) in order to gain control of that person's decision making. The process is accompanied by pressure, manipulation, fraud, duress, threats, or deceits.[77] If the influencer is successful in exerting undue influence, the end result is that the victim is harmed and the influencer benefits, most often financially through cash and property transfers, changes in ownership of accounts, or will beneficiary designation.

An influencer may seek to take advantage of the victim in other ways, such as through sexual exploitation, suspicious marriage, or by gaining housing or other personal benefits from a victim. The tactics of undue influence have been likened to those used by cult leaders, kidnappers in hostage situations, by sexual abusers who "groom" their victims, by perpetrators of domestic violence, and by charismatic leaders who create and sustain totalitarian regimes.[78] Older adults are more likely than younger adults to have financial assets which can make them attractive targets for undue influence.

Undue influence occurs behind closed doors in secrecy. It can be difficult to capture and describe. Upon review, the tactics and process of undue influence may seem obvious, but it is far more difficult to detect as it is transpiring.[79] There are usually no witnesses other than the victim and the influencer. There is seldom direct evidence. The victim of undue influence may not be able to clearly state what has happened or be aware that something untoward has happened. The victim may also deny the abuse or defend the influencer because of the existing relationship.[80]

The victim may be able to recite the details of their undue influence situation without understanding that they are being harmed. One victim, a retired chief financial officer for a

The "Caring" Son Case

A son was living with his father who was in his 80s and physically frail but mentally sound. He convinced his father to give him $8,000 per month because "I'm taking care of you." He would not allow two other siblings to visit saying their father was too ill and weak to receive visitors. He told his father, "Well the other kids won't help. They never visit. I'm the only one who cares about you. You'd end up in a nursing home if I wasn't here." After the father died, it was learned that the son had also induced his father to make a will leaving the family home to him as well as all his stocks and bank accounts.

multinational company, was the victim of a lottery scam. He said:

> Well, there is a lot of money going out. But, it is like an investment. I'm going to be receiving millions of dollars in return soon. And besides, they are my friends now and want to help me.[81]

B. Legal Perspective on Undue Influence

Historically, undue influence is a complex and poorly defined legal concept, one that remains difficult to translate into legal, clinical, or scientific terms. Little empirical research exists to guide clinicians in their assessment of undue influence.[82] As a result, states have for the most part relied upon case law. Many state statutes refer to the term "undue influence" without providing a definition.

Two legal models stand out as providing legal frameworks for considering undue influence. The Restatement of Contracts and the S-O-D-R model.

Restatement of Contracts

The *Restatement of Contracts*, a nonbinding but widely recognized and cited legal authority in common law, defines undue influence as follows:

"Undue influence is unfair persuasion of a party who is under the domination of the person exercising the persuasion or who by virtue of the relationship between them is justified in assuming that the person will not act in a manner inconsistent with his welfare. The Restatement goes on to say:

> If a party's manifestation of assent is induced by undue influence by the other party, the contract is voidable by the victim."[83]

This doctrine is akin to doctrines relating to fraud and duress. It may be alleged in legal challenges to the execution of a will, entering contracts or conveyance of property, and a means to financial or sexual abuse and even homicide.[84]

The S-O-D-R Model

The "SODR model, found in a handful of states, was designed to help courts determine whether to deny probate of a will based upon the theory of undue influence. "SODR" factors are:

- **S**usceptibility to undue influence
- **O**pportunity to influence
- **D**isposition to influence, and
- **R**esult coveted by the influencer.

Some states have adopted the SODR factors with modifications.

C. Clinical Frameworks for Understanding Undue Influence

Several professionals have proposed model frameworks that outline the main features of undue influence. These models are not mutually exclusive; generally, they complement each other.

The earliest clinical model for understanding undue influence was developed by Margaret Singer, PhD, a noted psychologist who worked with cult victims. She focused on the tactics that are used by undue influencers on their victims including creating isolation and a siege mentality, inducing dependency, promoting a sense of powerlessness, manipulating fears and vulnerabilities and keeping the victim unaware and uniformed. [85]

Bennet Blum, MD, JD a forensic psychiatrist, expanded on Singer's work. He developed the IDEAL Model:

- **I**solation
- **D**ependency
- **E**motional manipulation and/or exploitation of a vulnerability **A**cquiescence, and
- **L**oss. [86]

The Foreign "Friend" Case

Mrs. M's sister came to live with her because Mrs. M was getting forgetful and having difficulty managing her affairs. The sister observed Mrs. M speaking on the phone in a secretive manner several times a day. Mrs. M would not tell her sister who the caller was or what the call was about. Later, the sister learned that Mrs. M was talking to her "dear friend" who lived in a different country and who was going to make certain that Mrs. M received a million dollars if only she would send more money. It was a lottery scam. By the time the sister put a stop to the payments, over $80,000 was already lost.

The SCAM model, developed by neuropsychologist Susan Bernatz, PhD closely parallels the SODR model and draws from the Singer and Blum models. It focuses on:

- **S**usceptibility of victim
- **C**onfidential relationships between victims and abusers
- **A**ctive procurement of assets, and
- **M**onetary loss.

Dr. Bernatz provides both social influence conditions and also factors that contribute to the victim's susceptibility as well as the influencer's "active procurement" of legal or financial transactions. [87]

The Undue Influence Wheel, developed by social worker Bonnie Brandl and attorneys Candace Heisler and Lori Stiegel, focuses on undue influence tactics most often used to accomplish financial exploitation. The wheel is based on the assumption that undue influence has parallels to domestic violence, stalking, and sexual assault in which predatory perpetrators "groom" victims to gain power and control.[88]

Undue Influence Wheel
Common Tactics

In addition to the models already discussed, the British Columbia Law Institute issued a guide for attorneys and notaries that focuses on recognizing undue influence and taking practical steps when preparing wills. This guidebook helps lawyers and notaries recognize "red flags."[89]

CUIST: A Screening Tool for Undue Influence

To date, no universally accepted definitive formal assessment tool with ratings of severity and conclusions/diagnosis has been created in the legal context or the clinical context. However, the *California Undue Influence Screening Tool* (CUIST), presented in this chapter, draws from qualitative research, the legal and psychosocial literatures, and the work of Singer, Blum, Bernatz, Brandl, Heisler and Stiegel models described above as well as the Restatement of Contracts and SODR. It is structured around California legislation enacted in 2013 which outlines four elements of undue influence, consistent with research findings, and provides examples of each in the law: vulnerability of the victim; influencer's apparent authority; actions or tactics used by the influencer; and equity of the result.[90]

The tool helps identify, organize, and understand actions suggestive of undue influence. It helps protective services workers, attorneys, and others collect and organize facts and evidence, to evaluate the strength of a case for undue influence and to help decide if that theory should be pursued. Because it is a *screening* tool, it does not provide ratings of severity or a conclusory diagnosis. [91]

CUIST is a guide to gaining more clarity in alleged or actual undue influence situations. It uses plain, lay language that is jargon-free and evidence-based which permits the tool to be used by various professional groups as well as lay people. While the definition and elements of undue influence may be defined differently in each state, they will bear more resemblance than differences to the California Undue Influence Screening Tool, thus potentially making the tool useful anywhere.

UNDUE INFLUENCE SCREENING TOOL

California Influence Screening Tool (CUIST)[92]

Client's Name: ______________________________ **Date:** ____________________

The purpose of CUIST is to aid Adult Protective Service personnel screen for suspected undue influence. Undue influence means excessive persuasion that causes another person to act or refrain from acting by overcoming that person's free will and results in inequity.[93] CUIST is divided four categories: Client Vulnerability, Influencer's Authority/Power, Actions/Tactics, and Unfair/Improper Outcomes. Check all the factors that apply to the victim's circumstances and provide examples.

Client's Vulnerability	Examples / Comments
☐ Poor or declining health or physical disability ☐ Depends on others for help or care ☐ Problems with hearing, vision, or speaking Problems with memory ☐ Problems communicating and understanding Does not understand consequences of decisions Developmental disability ☐ Dependent or passive behavior ☐ Emotional distress (e.g., grief, anxiety, fear, depression) Language/literacy barriers ☐ Isolated from others ☐ Lives in chaotic or dysfunctional environment ☐ Influencer knew or should have known of person's vulnerability Other (please specify): ☐ No apparent vulnerability	

Influencer Authority/Position of Power	Examples / Comments
☐ Stands in a position of trust, authority, or confidence resulting from: ☐ Intimate/family relationship ☐ Caregiver ☐ Neighbor ☐ Professional standing (e.g., legal professional, spiritual adviser, health care professional, real estate agent, banker, accountant) ☐ Legal authority (e.g., power of attorney, conservatorship or guardianship, trust, representative payee) ☐ Controls elder's finances ☐ Immigration sponsor ☐ Landlord or long-term care facility operator ☐ Predatory salesperson (e.g., telemarketer, annuity company, lottery) ☐ Has access to client's home/possessions, finances, documents, or private information (e.g., legal/immigration status, sexual orientation/identity ☐ Other (please specify): ☐ No apparent authority, power, or access to assets and information	

Actions or Tactics	Examples / Comments
☐ Manipulates or controls the client's access to food, sleep, medication or personal care	
☐ Makes promises to help the client get rich	
☐ Makes false claims or promises, or misrepresents self (e.g., claims to be an expert)	
☐ Professionals or paid caregivers involve clients in their personal lives or ask for gifts/loans	
☐ Controls access to information	
☐ Isolates from visitors, telephone/computer, or mail	
☐ Instills distrust and fear (e.g., nursing home placement, abandonment, threats of violence, "poisons relationships")	
☐ Moves into client's residence or changes their residence	
☐ Changes clients' usual providers (e.g., physicians, lawyers, bankers, accountants)	
☐ Makes frequent/repeated requests that benefit the influencer	
☐ Pressures during periods of distress, illness, transition	
☐ Uses affection, sex, intimidation or coercion	
☐ Rushes client to make decisions secretly and at inappropriate times and places	
☐ Solicits or encourages gifts, loans, bequests, or cash	
☐ Other (Please specify:	
☐ No apparent use of actions or tactics described above	

Unfair or Improper Outcome(s)	Examples / Comments
☐ Economic losses (e.g., money, property, investments) ☐ Changes in prior intent, conduct, or practices (e.g., new beneficiaries on wills; new signatories on bank accounts, changes in property ownership, changes to estate plans or charitable contributions) ☐ Excessive gifts, payments, or donations in light of length and nature of relationship ☐ Loss of home or residence, or eviction Deterioration of home and environment ☐ Loss of control of credit cards, bank accounts, or property Identity theft ☐ Unexplained physical decline or injury including weight loss, physical function ☐ Negative mental or emotional changes including depression, loss of will to live, suicidal thoughts ☐ Violation of rights (e.g., to live where one wants, to marry or divorce, agree to or refuse treatment) ☐ Other (please specify): ☐ No apparent unfair or improper outcomes	

Summary
Check the following boxes that you believe apply to this client: ☐ Victim appears to be vulnerable. ☐ Suspected influencer appears to have power or authority over the client. ☐ Suspected influencer has taken steps suggestive of undue influence. ☐ Influencer's actions appear to have resulted in unfair, improper, or suspicious outcome.
Concluding Notes:

VII. Lawyer Assessment of Capacities

Lawyers must make capacity judgments in their everyday practice, either formally or informally, about two matters: first, whether a prospective client can enter into a contract for the attorney's services; and second, whether the client has the ability to understand and complete the specific legal transaction(s) under consideration.

This chapter outlines the lawyer's task of observation, legal analysis, and capacity judgment. For many, if not most clients, these will be the only necessary steps, because clinical consultation or assessment will not be needed to reach a firm conclusion about capacities in most cases. The counseling skills and decision support strategies described in Chapter IV provide a necessary foundation for this assessment process by ensuring that clients are seen under circumstances that support and enhance their capacity. The remaining chapters describe the process of obtaining and using an informal clinical consultation or a formal clinical assessment, should the lawyer believe that step is necessary prior to forming a final conclusion about the client's legal capacity.

A. The Capacity Worksheet

The process described below focuses on key signs and factors to consider in an assessment of legal capacity. The process outlined is meant to structure and record observations leading to a legal judgment that is sufficiently comprehensive in scope, systematic in process, accountable if challenged, and documented. This process is not intended to be a validated clinical measure of capacity; rather it is a tool for collecting and organizing relevant observations.

The process is geared to blend in naturally to the case interview process, rather than adding a new costly element. The Worksheet at the end of this chapter essentially systematizes and documents what the lawyer already does implicitly. The Worksheet is designed to be used by the lawyer either during the client interview as a note-taking device, or immediately afterwards as an analytic tool.

Unavoidable capacity determinations: Does the client have the capacity to contract for my services?

1. **Does the client have the capacity to complete the legal transaction?**
2. **Are there supports and services that would address concerns about capacity and allow my client to contract for my services and/or complete the legal transaction?**

Lawyers need a conceptually sound and consistent process for answering these questions.

WORKSHEET PART A: Observing Signs of Possible Diminished Capacities

There is no single indicator that provides a consistent, clear signal that an older adult is functioning with diminished capacities. However, there are markers that, when considered together, may reflect diminished capacities. These signs are not proof of diminished capacity. If these signs are present in sufficient number and/or severity, they may indicate a need for further evaluation of capacity by an independent professional.

In noting potential signs of incapacity, it is important to keep in mind that the focus is on decisional abilities rather than on cooperativeness or affability. It may be challenging to disentangle one's reactions to a client's interpersonal style from observations of the client's cognitive, emotional, or behavioral problems.

If a client is a returning one, it is critical to consider the history of interactions and pay attention to changes in behavior and functioning. A baseline of what is typical for any particular person is extremely helpful in assessing current decisional abilities. Be sensitive to gradual or sudden changes in functioning among returning clients.

Finally, it is useful to be sensitive to societal stereotypes about aging, i.e., ageism. Aging stereotypes may be positive, idealizing old age; or negative, perhaps including the assumption that aging and diminished capacity are synonymous, or an assumption that sensory impairments in hearing or vision imply cognitive impairment. Such beliefs can influence an appraisal of capacity.

During the course of an interview, the attorney should be aware of specific signs that serve as "red flags;" possible indicators of neurological or psychiatric illness that could diminish capacity. Most of the red flags will be observed during the interview or reported by third parties such as family members. It will not be necessary (and in most cases not appropriate) to use psychological screening instruments during preliminary capacity assessments.

During and immediately after a client interview, the attorney can document the signs observed, and also make notations about the nature and severity of these signs on the Worksheet.

Possible Cognitive Signs of Incapacity

Short-term Memory Loss

A client quickly may forget information discussed in the interview, repeating the same statements or asking the same question multiple times, with no indication that she or he has done so more than once. Also, while the client can discuss events from 10 years to 20 years ago, there may be more difficulty describing events of the past few days or weeks. For example, the client may be able to engage in brief casual conversation, such as a five-minute conversation about the weather or sports, but have trouble going beyond that in detail and begin to repeat questions already asked or forget your name or the purpose of the visit. The ability to engage in such small talk can lead family who live out of town to say that an impaired older adult "sounds just fine on the phone.

Communication Barriers

A great deal can be learned by observing how the client uses language and communicates ideas. For example, a client may have repeated difficulty finding a particular word or naming common items even if they can talk about the item. A certain amount of word loss is normal for the aging brain but may be significant if recurring. For example, she may say "I brought my thing with the papers in it" instead of "I brought my notebook." A common "cover" tactic for older adults with memory or communication problems is to defer to others excessively when asked direct questions, perhaps saying "My wife handles all the appointments, you'd have to ask her if we went," or "I hardly ever call my own phone number; my son would remember because he uses it."

Clients who are asked direct questions may have trouble staying on the topic of interest, frequently shifting to discussion of unrelated issues, or moving erratically or nonsensically between topics. Such problems can indicate trouble organizing thoughts such as is found in frontal dementia or in thought disorder (e.g., psychotic thinking). Repeated difficulty finding words and vague or disorganized language may indicate an inability to communicate a clear decision or to comprehend important information relevant to the decision.

Comprehension Challenges

It is important to explore the client's comprehension of information. Be sure to ask open ended rather than yes/no questions. Difficulty repeating back or paraphrasing simple concepts is indicative of problems in comprehension. Repeated questioning could indicate poor memory or poor comprehension. Many people with poor memory can paraphrase information immediately, while individuals with poor comprehension will have trouble even with this.

Lack of Mental Flexibility

A client may lack the capacity to understand or even acknowledge multiple alternatives or viewpoints other than her or his own, or have difficulty comprehending and adjusting to changes. This is different from simply being stubborn in that someone who is stubborn can typically acknowledge that other perspectives exist and can provide reasons for not choosing them. For example, a stubborn person may not want to change a will for particular reasons, whereas an older adult lacking in mental flexibility may exhibit a general fear of making any changes for very vague reasons.

Math & Financial Challenges

These may manifest themselves in multiple ways:

- Problems with Everyday Arithmetic--difficulties with simple math problems that the client would normally be able to do. The client may present signs suggesting impairment in financial management abilities more broadly, e.g., lack of awareness of their own financial assets or debts.

- Decreased Understanding of Financial Concepts-- such as interest rates, medical deductibles, or net assets.
- Decreased Comprehension of Ordinary Financial Document-- such as bank statements or bill statements indicating past due amounts.
- Diminished Awareness of Financial Risks-- for example, the client may have trouble identifying key risks in an investment proposal that fits the description "too good to be true," or the likely scam nature of a promised reward for money transfers. The client is focused on benefits/return and not risk.

Disorientation

Disorientation can occur relative to space, time, or location. For example, a long-time client may have difficulty navigating through the attorney's office building spatially or may get lost driving to the office even if he or she has been there several times over many years (spatial orientation). Once there, the client may not be able to identify where he or she is (orientation to place). The client may also not be aware of what time it is or what year it is, perhaps making references to events from several years ago as if the events were current (orientation to time).

Possible ***Emotional*** *Signs of Incapacity*

Significant Emotional Distress

A client may be persistently emotionally distressed during an interview or across interviews, beyond typical emotions expected given the circumstances, such that the individual's emotional state makes it very difficult to address the relevant legal questions. For example, the client may appear extremely anxious, tearful, or seem depressed and appear to have no energy and respond very slowly to questions.

Emotional Lability/Inappropriateness

Rather than a steady emotional state, a client may show an extremely wide range of emotions during an interview (perhaps moving quickly from laughter to tears). Alternatively, a client may express feelings that seem highly inconsistent with what he or she is discussing (laughter when discussing death of a spouse, tears of distress while professing to be happy).

Possible ***Behavioral*** *Signs of Incapacity*

Delusions

Delusions are beliefs that are unlikely to be true, such as a belief that neighbors or the government are spying on oneself. Delusional thinking may be manifest more generally in expressions of feeling frightened or unsafe. Presence of delusions may call into question the extent to which decisions are founded on sound reasoning.

For example, consider a delusional nursing home resident who stops eating because of beliefs that the food is being poisoned. It is important not to discount delusions without investigation. The concerns of older adults about relatives or facility staff stealing money or possessions from them are unfortunately often inaccurately labeled as delusions.

Hallucinations

Hallucinations are sensory experiences in the absence of physical stimuli that could be responsible for such experiences, such as hearing voices that no one else can hear. They are often auditory or visual, but can involve the other senses: smell, touch, and/or taste. An example is an older adult who seems to be having a conversation with another person who is not there. As with delusions, hallucinations may call into question the extent to which a decision is reality-based. However, it should be noted that high functioning older adults who are recently widowed and grieving sometimes report hearing a deceased spouse call their name or briefly seeing their image. Also, significant hearing or vision problems can place an older adult at risk for sensory misperceptions. When combined with isolation and anxiety, such misperceptions may appear hallucinatory or delusional in quality.

Poor Grooming/Hygiene

Individuals who are experiencing cognitive difficulties or serious emotional problems may not brush their hair, shave, or shower regularly, or have other grooming issues. For example, along with irregular bathing or shaving, a relatively common behavior among older adults with dementia is to wear multiple layers of clothing, perhaps several shirts or multiple pairs of pants. Attention to the appearance, clothing, and smell of a client gives clues to possible mental status changes.

Markedly Inappropriate Social Behaviors

When these are uncharacteristic of the person, they can be indicative of brain pathology. These may include a loss of empathy and other interpersonal skills, a loss of inhibitions, a marked lack of judgment, or an uncharacteristic lack of interest (apathy), which can be mistaken for depression.

Functioning Beyond the Office

Observations in the office setting are obviously quite limited. If the lawyer has the ability to interview clients in their home setting, there is a definite advantage in being able to see some of their functioning in their natural and familiar environment. The lawyer may in the natural course of contact with clients—and family members with whom your client has permitted communication—learn other information about the client's level of functioning at home, particularly with respect to "activities of daily living," (ADLs) and "instrumental activities of daily living" (IADLs).

Such information may or may not be relevant to capacity. For example, an inability to write checks to pay the bill may be merely a physical deficit (and thus have nothing to do with decisional capacity), or it may be a result of failing to remember payment obligations or how to understand a bill (and thus be quite relevant to capacity for certain legal tasks).

Observations of the home environment can be valuable, for example, revealing unsanitary conditions or hoarding; lack of heating or cooling; piling up of bills or medicines; or signs of difficulty obtaining and preparing food. Together such signs signal at least a need for home services but also a possible dementing disorder. In any case, additional information regarding client functioning in the home and community rounds out the total picture of the client abilities and deficits. The worksheet provides a space for recording any such information about the client's functioning beyond the office setting.

ADLs	IADLs
Dressing	Grocery shopping & meal preparation
Bathing	Driving
Toileting	Housework
Eating	Managing money
Walking	Managing medication
Transferring between bed/chair	Using telephone, mail, and email

Undue Influence

See Chapter VI for a deeper dive into undue influence, and if there is any question about its presence, use the California Undue Influence Screening Tool in that chapter.

Mitigating/Qualifying Factors in Assessing Signs of Diminished Capacity

Mitigating/qualifying factors indicate a need for alternative action, be it a referral to a physician, adjusting the approach to communication, or scheduling another time when the client is functioning better. The American Bar Association's *PRACTICAL Tool* is a useful resource for reviewing these factors and exploring possible decision supports.[94]

Stress; Grief; Depression; Recent Stressful Events

A client may at times seem confused, unable to pay attention to instructions, or unable to make decisions. It is important to ascertain stresses in the client's life that could cause anxiety, depression, or inability to act. These potential signs of diminished capacity could go away when the transient stresses are alleviated.

Reversible Medical Factors

Signs of disorientation and confusion could be due to a host of medical conditions and medication factors that are reversible. Some common causes are related to medications: adverse medication reaction, interactions among too many medications (polypharmacy), and taking medications incorrectly. Also, older adults can be extremely sensitive to dietary insufficiency–inadequate nutrition, hydration, and deficiency in certain vitamins in the diet can lead to temporary cognitive changes. Further, persistent pain may impact cognition. A referral to a physician, preferably a geriatrician prior to further action may be indicated.

Indeed, if the client has not had a complete physical in the past year, referral is always worthwhile.

Normal Fluctuations in Mental Ability in Older Adults

Mental status may vary according to the time of day. Clinicians have learned that it is often better to test older adults in mid-morning when the individual is most alert.

Hearing and Vision Loss

Losses in hearing and vision are normal in aging. Diminished functioning in the senses should not be generalized to mental incapacity. The amount and type of loss varies from person to person. Older adults learn ways to compensate for these losses. However, problems in hearing and vision can sometimes present a picture that the older client cannot attend, focus, or provide appropriate responses to questions. See Chapter IV. for accommodations attorneys can make for clients experiencing hearing and vision loss.

Social/Environmental Factors

Individuals perform best in environments they feel comfortable and safe in. The lawyer's office itself may be a stressor, especially if it is not designed to be "elder friendly" – accommodating to any disability. It is important to assess how well your office is designed. Environments are also social, so other family or friends who accompany your client may themselves influence your client negatively or positively. Meeting with the client privately for at least part of the interview process is vital to accurate assessment.[95]

Cultural and Other Differences

Mental abilities can be influenced by a person's education, life and job-related experiences, and sometimes socio-economic background. The styles and strategies used in mental performances can be further influenced by the client's gender, personality, lifestyle choices, value system, and eccentricities. In addition, cultural and ethnic traditions in approaching personal, family, and medical issues may vary. From this perspective, the range of cognitive functions that is considered normal among older adults is large. These individual differences are important and need to be taken into account in evaluating your own implicit biases and in evaluating potential mental capacity of the older clients.

Other Decision Supports

Beside mitigating obvious problems, it is important to thoroughly and creatively explore other decision supports that may maximize the client's ability to make their own decisions. See Chapter II for further discussion of supporting decision-making.

Supported Decision-Making

- **Encompasses a series of relationships, practices, arrangements and agreements,**
- **of more or less formality and intensity,**
- **designed to assist an individual with a disability to make and communicate to others decisions about the individual's life.**

WORKSHEET PART B: Evaluating a Client's Understanding in Relation to Legal Elements of Capacity

Observation of signs of diminished capacity is only an initial step for the attorney evaluating a client's capacity. The next and more substantive step per the Worksheet is to evaluate the client's legal capacity specifically for the transaction or situation at issue. This requires a direct comparison of the client's understanding with each of the functional elements of capacity set out in statute or case law for the transaction or situation at hand.

Chapter V covers the standards of capacity for several common actions and transactions for which capacity questions may arise. Use them in the assessment process when they apply.

The client's decisional process will be implicit and intuitive in part, as well as explicit and conscious. The attorney's role is to present information, answer and ask questions, gently probe and query, and weigh client responses and thought processes. In addition, with client consent or in accordance with the rules of ethics, the attorney could solicit information from family members and other collateral sources, including fellow professionals. The decisional process may occur over the course of one or several meetings with the client. Ultimately, the attorney must form a judgment about the client's understanding of the respective legal elements of transaction at issue, utilizing the decision supports that can be brought to bear.

WORKSHEET PART C: Consider Task-Specific Factors in the Model Rules

The six task-specific factors described below derive from Comment 6 to Rule 1.14 of the Model Rules of Professional Conduct. The Rule and Comment have not been adopted in every state, yet they merit consideration because they are clinically relevant for assessment and their consideration fits naturally within the client interview:

1. *The client's ability to articulate reasoning leading to a decision.* The client should be able to state the basis for his or her decision. The stated reasons for the decision should be consistent with the client's overall stated goals and objectives.

2. *Variability of state of mind.* Fluctuating levels of the individual's cognitive functioning pose a challenge but not necessarily an insurmountable barrier to capacity. For example, a client with short-term memory issues may forget about a decision made a few days ago, but on revisiting the question, the client may express the same choice each time. Or, a client demanding an extremely uncharacteristic change in their legal affairs, after a cooling off period, may revert to their more characteristic values and wishes.

3. *Ability to appreciate consequences of a decision.* For example, does a client recognize that without a given medical decision, he or she may risk physical decline or even death–or without a legal challenge to an eviction, he or she may be without a place to live. A person with capacity chooses to take a particular risk; a person lacking capacity just happens to take that risk.

4. *The substantive fairness of the decision.* While lawyers must normally defer to client decisions, a lawyer nonetheless cannot simply look the other way if an older individual, or someone else, is being taken advantage of in a blatantly unfair transaction. To do so could defeat the very dignity and autonomy the lawyer seeks to enhance, and thus fairness is one element to balance. Of course, judging fairness risks the interjection of one's own beliefs and values, so extreme caution is required.

When the desired legal plan conforms to conventional notions of fairness– e.g., equitable distribution of assets among all children–or the plan is consistent with the lawyer's longstanding knowledge of the client and family, then capacity concerns tend to wane proportionately. Capacity may be diminished yet still adequate for a legal transaction deemed to be very low risk in the context of conventional fairness.

5. *The consistency of a decision with the known long-term commitments and values of the client.* The decision normally should reflect the client's lifelong or long-term perspective. This will be easier to determine if the lawyer-client relationship is long-standing. At the same time, individuals can change their values framework as they age. The distinction is important.

6. *Irreversibility of the decision.* The law tends to give greater scrutiny to decisions with significant consequences that cannot be reversed. Similarly, in counseling the client, the lawyer should ensure the client understands the consequences and their irreversibility of such a transaction. For example, a will is changeable after execution, at least in theory, but the giving of a large gift in the present normally will not be reversible.

Of these six factors, the first three are "functional" in the sense that they reflect the cognitive functioning of the individual. These may be supported by observation of the presence or lack of signs described previously. The latter three are "substantive" in that they look at the content and nature of the decision itself. The latter three factors may be thought of as substantive "levers" that modulate a kind of sliding scale of capacity. The greater the concerns under the latter three substantive variables (fairness, consistency with commitments, irreversibility), the greater the level of functioning demanded under the first three variables (ability to articulate reasoning, variability of state of mind, and appreciation of consequences). In other words, the higher the risk (as measured by the client's own values, the finality, and fairness), the more one must probe to ensure decisional capacity.

The paradigm has no direct evidence-based validation in the psychological or medical literature, although the paradigm is consistent with the psychological models previously described in Chapter III, emphasizing functional and interactive (i.e., substantive) aspects of capacity. The paradigm originated in an ethical analysis by Peter Margulies of the threshold for protective action, enhanced by an appreciation of the realities of legal counseling.[96]

A key strength is that the factors Margulies enumerated blend quite seamlessly with the kind of issues that lawyers would typically discuss in counseling clients. In that respect, the factors are very user-friendly for lawyers and amenable to easy documentation in the lawyer's notes. A careful weighing and balancing of these factors along with the specific elements of legal capacity for the transaction at hand will assist the lawyer to make a preliminary judgment of capacity.

WORKSHEET PART D: Performing the Legal Analysis and Categorizing the Legal Judgment

In making a capacity judgment at this stage (without resorting to clinical consultation or formal assessment), an attorney will need to weigh all the data obtained as a whole. The completed worksheet summarizes the lawyer's observations regarding cognitive, emotional, and behavioral functioning in Part A; the presence of any mitigating factors affecting the observations and the availability of supportive resources to maximize the client's capacity under Part B; the client's decisional functioning in comparison to the applicable legal tests as queried in Part D; and your assessment of the task specific factors recommended under Part D of the Worksheet.

With these data, the lawyer should make a categorical assignment of the fit between the client's abilities and the legal capacity at issue. Unfortunately, there is no simple score that will help the attorney easily to arrive at a conclusion. The conclusion is ultimately a professional judgment that is aided by the systematic consideration of signs of incapacity, the client's understanding of the legal transaction, and the factors laid out in the Model Rule. In integrating these sources of data to form a conclusion, the attorney may consider the classification schema in the box below:

Preliminary Screening Conclusions

- **No or minimal** evidence of diminished capacity
- **Mild** – There is some evidence of diminished capacity
- **More than Mild** – There is substantial but inconclusive evidence of client capacity

If the attorney feels uncertain as to whether the observed problems represent "mild" versus "more than mild" issues, this would be an indication to consult with a clinician as described in Chapter VIII.

B. Documenting the Capacity Judgment

As in other client matters, the attorney should document his or her observations and assessment regarding client capacity. The worksheet provides that documentation, although it may be advisable to further summarize key observations, conclusions, and reasonings in a case note, either in the space provided at the end of the worksheet or elsewhere in a case summary. In cases where the additional steps of consultation with a mental health professional or referral for formal assessment are necessary, the worksheet provides a first level of assessment. Once additional steps are taken (as described in Chapters VIII), the lawyer should document further analysis, judgment, and final disposition in the case file.

Videotaping as Documentation?

The question is often asked whether videotaping of the client completing a legal transaction, such as a will signing or being questioned just before the transaction is a good idea. Experienced practitioners have come to different conclusions on this question. In selected cases, videotape evidence of a client explaining his or her reasons behind a particular dispositive provision can provide a deterrence to a contest. But, there are several arguments against videotaping the client's execution of a document:

- Videotaping may in fact exaggerate the client's deficits in decision making;
- Unless the attorney videotapes all clients, the fact of videotaping may itself be used to raise doubts of capacity;
- The videotape cannot be edited to remove portions for any reason without risking ethical or legal violation of evidence tampering prohibitions.

C. Taking Actions Following Informal Capacity Assessment

Following a preliminary capacity assessment, an attorney may need to weigh different courses of action. In the majority of cases, presumably there will be no issues of diminished capacity and the attorney can proceed with the legal representation without further concern. In the case of "mild concerns" about capacity, the attorney should explore all possible decisional supports to enable representation to proceed. Also consider a referral for a *geriatric medical evaluation* to ensure there are no medical problems which may be transiently affecting capacity and for which resolution could remove any lingering concerns.

In cases involving more than mild capacity concerns, even with decision supports, or if supports are unavailable, the attorney should consider a general geriatric work-up as recommended for mild concerns. At the same time, consultation with a clinician for guidance, or formal referral for clinical assessment should be considered. After taking such external steps, the attorney then can decide the best course of action concerning the representation.

In situations where capacity signs are severe, representation by the attorney may be impossible. Formal clinical assessment should still be recommended. If withdrawal from direct representation is necessary, be sure to take all reasonable steps to protect the client's interests. If a client-lawyer relationship already exists before capacity becomes an issue, then protective action may be ethically appropriate under Model Rule 1.14(b).

A formal evaluation of capacity by a clinician will be useful in supporting these actions. Communication with the client about the capacity issues, as well as with family members and significant others where appropriate under the rules of confidentiality, may be warranted to protect the client's legal interests and to reduce the risk of exploitation.

D. Caution Against Attorney Use of Psychological Instruments

Cognitive screening instruments have enjoyed wide acceptance and use in clinical settings, mainly because of their brevity and simplicity in administering, scoring, and interpreting. Several brief mental status questionnaires have been developed, the most well-known of which is the 30-item Mini-Mental Status Examination (MMSE), although others are widely used, too. See the Cognitive Screening tests summarized in Appendix 1.

The MMSE provides a quick but blunt assessment of overall cognitive mental status. It assesses orientation, attention, registration and immediate recall, language, and the ability to follow simple verbal and written commands. It provides a total score that places the individual on a 30-point scale of cognitive function. In clinical settings, the MMSE has been used to detect impairment, follow the course of an illness, monitor response to treatment, screen for cognitive disorders in epidemiological studies, and follow cognitive changes in clinical trials.

While this handbook argues that lawyers regularly engage in the legal assessment of capacity and should do so in a systematic manner, for a variety of reasons addressed below, it is generally not appropriate for attorneys to use more formal clinical assessment instruments, such as the MMSE.

Lack of Training. Lawyers generally do not have the clinical education and training needed to administer these tests.

Limited Yield. For an attorney, the information yield of psychological screening instruments is very limited. At best, screening test scores will indicate that further psychological evaluation is needed, which could often be better determined on the basis of careful observation and a thorough interview.

Over-Reliance. There is a danger of over-reliance on single test scores. Single test scores can unfortunately appear to be objectively and numerically precise. A multidimensional approach to clinical assessment is considered the gold standard for formal assessment. Decisions should not be made on the basis of a single test score.

False Negatives and False Positives. Screening exams such as the MMSE pose a risk of producing both false positives and false negatives in conclusions about mental deficits related to relevant tasks. For example, a client mobility problem (e.g., arthritis) may have a reduced MMSE score related to difficulty drawing pentagons or folding a paper. This deficit has little relevance to the ability to prepare an advance directive. Such a conclusion would be a "false positive." On the other hand, an individual who demonstrates excellent performance on the MMSE (knows the date, has good memory) but has a specific focused and unfounded delusion about a family member, which represents an acute psychosis, may lack testamentary capacity despite the high score. This is a "false negative"

Practice Effects. When cognitive screening tests are used more than once, familiarity with the test can improve performance, even though one's cognitive functioning has not improved.

Lack of Specificity to Legal Incapacity. In a number of studies, cognitive screening alone has been found lacking sensitivity or specificity to many decisional tasks, such as medical decision making.[97]

Attorney Assessment Worksheet

This worksheet is from *Assessment of Older Adults with Diminished Capacities: A Handbook for Lawyers (2020)*

It has been reproduced with minor changes from *Assessment of Older Adults with Diminished Capacity: A Handbook for Lawyers.*

Please read and review the Handbook prior to using the worksheet.

Client: ______________________________ **Date of Interview:** ____________________

Attorney:______________________________ **Place of Interview:**____________________

A. Observational Signs

►Cognitive Functioning	Examples
Short-term Memory Problems	▪ Repeats questions frequently ▪ Forgets what is discussed within 15-30 min. ▪ Cannot remember events of past few days
Language/Communication Problems	▪ Difficulty finding words frequently ▪ Vague language, Disorganized ▪ Trouble staying on topic ▪ Bizarre statements or reasoning ▪ Difficulty using phone, email and/or other forms of communication
Comprehension Problems	▪ Difficulty repeating simple concepts ▪ Repeated questioning
Lack of Mental Flexibility	▪ Difficulty comparing alternatives ▪ Difficulty adjusting to changes
Disorientation	▪ Trouble navigating office ▪ Gets lost coming to office ▪ Confused about day/time/year/season
Financial Management Abilities:	
▪ Problems with Everyday Arithmetic	▪ More difficulty calculating: Sum of loose change Feet to inches conversion Tip in a restaurant
▪ Decreased Understanding of Financial Concepts	▪ More difficulty understanding: Health care concepts like medical deductible Terms like interest rate, lien, and joint liability
▪ Decreased Comprehension of Ordinary Financial Documents	▪ More difficulty: Identifying a bill that is overdue and needs prompt attention Finding details in a bank statement Completing sections of a check register

▪ Diminished Awareness of Financial Risks	▪ Trouble identifying key risk in investment proposal ▪ Overly focused on benefits/return, not risk
▶ Emotional Functioning	
Emotional Distress	▪ Anxious ▪ Tearful/distressed ▪ Excited/pressured/manic
Emotional Lability	▪ Moves quickly between laughter and tears ▪ Feelings inconsistent with topic
▶ Behavioral Functioning	
Delusions	▪ Feels others out "to get" him/her, spying or organized against him/her ▪ Fearful, feels unsafe
Hallucinations	▪ Appears to hear or talk to things not there ▪ Appears to see things not there ▪ Misperceives things
Poor Grooming/Hygiene	▪ Unusually unclean/unkempt in appearance ▪ Inappropriately dressed
Markedly Inappropriate Social Behavior	▪ Loss of empathy and interpersonal skills ▪ Lack of judgment; Loss of inhibition ▪ Lack of interest (apathy), which can be mistaken for depression
Other Observations + Notes from 3rd parties	
☐ **Potential Undue Influence – Use Undue Influence Screen**	

Mitigating/Qualifying Factors Affecting Observations	Ways to Address/Accommodate
Stress, grief, depression, recent events affecting stability of client	▪ Ask about recent events, losses ▪ Allow some time ▪ Refer to a mental health professional ▪ Help find support persons or groups ▪
Medical Factors	▪ Ask about nutrition, medications, hydration ▪ Refer to a physician
Time of Day Variability	▪ Ask if certain times of the day are best ▪ Try mid-morning appointment
Hearing and Vision Loss	▪ Assess ability to read or repeat simple information ▪ Adjust seating, lighting ▪ Use visual and hearing aids

Social/Environmental Factors	▪ High anxiety level in unfamiliar environment ▪ Presence of others causing stress ▪ Help find personal/social supports
Educational/Cultural/Ethnic Barriers	▪ Be aware of race, ethnicity, education, long-held values and traditions, and your own implicit biases ▪ Help find peer supporters
What other decision supports does the client need to maximize decision-making abilities?	

B. RELEVANT LEGAL ELEMENTS - The legal elements of capacity vary somewhat among states and should be modified as needed for your particular state.

What are the Legal Task(s) at Issue?	
What are the Capacity Elements of the Task(s)? This requires your state-specific research. (See Chapter V.)	**Notes on Client's Understanding/ Appreciation/Functioning Under Elements**

C. TASK SPECIFIC FACTORS IN PRELIMINARY EVALUATION OF CAPACITY

The more serious the concerns about the following factors… ⇨	**The higher the function needed in the following abilities…**
Is decision consistent with client's known long-term values or commitments?	Can client articulate reasoning leading to this decision?
Is the decision objectively fair? Will anyone be hurt by the decision?	Is client's decision consistent over time? Are primary values client articulates consistent over time?
Is the decision irreversible?	Can client appreciate consequences of his/her decision?

D. PRELIMINARY CONCLUSIONS ABOUT CLIENT CAPACITY

After evaluating A, B, and C above:

☐ **No or minimal** evidence of diminished capacity.	*Action:* Proceed with representation and transaction
☐ **Mild concerns** – Some evidence of diminished capacity, but less than substantial.	*Action Options:* (1) Proceed with representation/transaction. An associated note to the file may be helpful to document your conclusion. (2) Explore decision support strategies to reinforce capacity. (3) Consider medical referral if medical oversight lacking. (4) Consider consultation with mental health professional. (5) Consider referral for formal clinical assessment to substantiate conclusion, with client consent.
☐ **More than mild concerns** about capacity even with decision supports, or decision-support is not available.	*Action Options:* (1) Explore decision support strategies further to reinforce capacity. Clear documentation of concerns and actions contemplated or taken will be important here. (2) Medical referral if medical oversight lacking. (3) Consultation with mental health professional. (4) Refer for formal clinical assessment, with client consent.
☐ **Severe concerns** – Client clearly lacks capacity to proceed with representation and transaction	*Action Options:* (1) The representation cannot proceed, and alternative legal approaches must be taken (for example, working with family members). (2) Referral to mental health professional to confirm conclusion. (3) Do not proceed with case; or withdraw, after careful consideration of how to protect client's interests. (4) If an existing client, consider protective action consistent with MRPC 1.14(b).

Case Notes: Summarize key observations, application of relevant legal criteria, conclusions, and actions to be taken:

VIII. Referrals for Consultation or Formal Assessment

This chapter describes four key matters every lawyer needs to know: (A) the basic considerations relevant to seeking consultation or referral to a clinician for formal assessment; (B) how to select a clinician; (C) the elements or steps of any referral; and (D) how to communicate with the clinician doing the assessment.

A. Basic Considerations in Seeking Consultation or Referral

In transactional legal representations, three common scenarios can lead to the decision to seek professional consultation or to make a formal referral for assessment.

First, the attorney may have sufficiently strong concerns about the capacity of the client that it is important to seek clinical expertise and input on the issue before proceeding further or taking protective action as allowed in Rule 1.14(b). Second, in cases of ongoing or anticipated family or other conflict, the foresighted attorney may seek to preempt a future litigation (e.g., a will contest) by having the client undergo a capacity assessment prior to execution of the legal transaction (e.g., the will). Third, the attorney may have concerns about their client's risk factors for undue influence and seek clinical opinion on susceptibility.

Under the preliminary conclusions schema presented in preceding chapter, the lawyer may distinguish clients about which the attorney has (1) no or minimal concerns about capacity, (2) mild concerns, (3) more than mild concerns, or (4) severe concerns. The lawyer may find it helpful to contact a suitable clinician in situations where the attorney has *more than mild concerns* about diminished capacity. For clients for whom only *mild concern*, have arisen, further evaluation generally is not necessary, unless for example, the attorney concludes that interested third persons may challenge the legal transactions at some point, based upon allegations of mental incapacity. In these situations, the attorney may want to recommend formal evaluation of the client as a defensive measure.

Sometimes an attorney will seek a private consultation with a clinician to discuss and clarify specific capacity issues before proceeding further with representation. Disclosure of the attorney's concerns is private, at least at this stage of the process, and does not involve the client. The Comment to Rule 1.14(b) provides explicit recognition of such external consultations, indicating that it is proper for attorneys to seek guidance from an "appropriate diagnostician" in cases where clients demonstrate diminished capacity.[98]

In other cases, an attorney may feel compelled by capacity concerns, litigation strategy, or other case circumstances to seek an independent formal capacity evaluation by a clinician. Such a decision is significant because it necessarily involves disclosure to the client of an attorney's concerns or litigation strategy and requires a client's consent to be evaluated. It represents a significant step by the attorney that can impact the attorney-client relationship in both positive and negative ways.

Decisions of this type, thus, will sometimes necessitate lengthy and forthright discussions with clients and family members.

This being said, such capacity evaluations and written reports are usually quite valuable because when conducted properly, they furnish objective cognitive and behavioral data and professional expertise to the attorney and the case. The opinions of a clinician can serve as evidence or be advisory in a number of important functions, outlined in the box, next page. At the same time, a formal assessment is not without danger, for there is always the potential adverse use of such an evaluation

Key Points

- **In most cases, it will not be necessary to consult with a clinician.**
- **Knowledge of clinical models of capacity can be useful.**
- **Many legal and clinical concepts of capacity are similar.**
- **There is consensus on clinical models of capacity.**

against the lawyer's client. Though the report may be protected under physician-patient privilege and attorney-client privilege when the client refuses to consent to disclosure, these privileges are variable under state law and subject to a host of exceptions and interpretations. Their protection from discovery in civil litigation is not absolute.[48]

On this point it should be emphasized that the clinical evaluation *need not result in a formal written report*. The lawyer may instruct the clinician to do the evaluation, and then to call the lawyer with preliminary, unwritten conclusions, after which the lawyer can state whether or not the clinician should commit the clinical opinion to writing.

In making a referral, it is important for the lawyer to recognize his or her own continuing role. Ultimately, the attorney determines whether the client has the capacity to consent to the legal transaction at hand. While the results of a clinical assessment generally will be a determining factor, client capacity is a *legal decision* and an inherent part of the lawyer-client relationship. Thus, the lawyer can use the assessment report as valuable—ideally conclusive—evidence, but still needs to "look behind" the report and make an independent judgment taking all factors into account.

Potential uses of clinical opinion regarding client capacity:

- **Expert testimony in a subsequent deposition or courtroom hearing.**
- **Clarification of the areas of diminished capacity and of retained strengths.**
- **Affirmation of the client's capacity.**
- **Justification of the attorney's capacity concerns to disbelieving clients and family members.**
- **Expert advice on strategies to compensate for identified mental deficits.**
- **Indication of the need for protective action.**
- **Recommendation for follow-up testing (anticipated restoration of capacity).**

B. Selecting a Clinician

Although the Comment to Rule 1.14(b) permits the lawyer to find an "appropriate diagnostician" it does not specify who is "appropriate." Of note, although the Model Rule refers to "diagnostician," a better term is clinician, as the process of capacity assessment involves more than a diagnosis, especially with the move away from merely making a diagnosis to describing cognitive and functional abilities.

Ideally, the most appropriate clinician would be a medical or mental health professional who is knowledgeable about the problems of late life, familiar with assessment approaches and instruments relevant to capacity issues, and has considerable experience conducting capacity assessments. Unfortunately, the number of professionals with ideal credentials is small.

Lawyers in rural or smaller communities may find it difficult to locate a psychiatrist or psychologist within reasonable driving distance. In this case, the lawyer may need to rely on local professional resources even if they are not ideal. A respected medical internist with a geriatric clientele may be appropriate.

A critical step in making a referral is to articulate clearly the area of referral expertise needed. Consider whether the client's impairment may stem from intellectual or developmental disability, mental illness, Alzheimer's or other type of dementia, or other possible medical cause. The expertise for examining these different etiologies can be quite different. For example, a neurologist may have expertise in problems associated with Alzheimer's disease (a cognitive illness) while a psychiatrist is likely to have more expertise in schizophrenia (a psychiatric illness). The more closely the expertise is matched to the underlying impairment, the more likely the diagnostician can accurately assess the client and provide needed answers.

When considering a referral, the lawyer should ascertain the qualifications of the assessor. Most medical professionals are "boarded" or have "added qualifications" in one or several specialty areas. Being boarded or having added qualifications means that the individual has obtained required

Key Professionals for Capacity Consultation or Referral	
Physician	**Any MD or DO**
Geriatrician	**MD specialist in aging**
Geriatric Psychiatrist or Geropsychologist	**Mental health specialists in aging**
Forensic Psychologist or Psychiatrist	**Mental health specialists in law**
Neurologist	**MD specialist in the brain functioning**
Neuropsychologist	**Psychologist specialist in cognitive testing**
Geriatric Assessment Team	**Multidisciplinary teams in aging**

training and education and passed an exam. Relevant medical boarded specialties include geriatric medicine, psychiatry, neurology, geriatric psychiatry, and forensic psychiatry.

In psychology, there is increasing specialization although the boarding process has not been as important as in medicine. A small number of psychologists are boarded by the American Board of Professional Psychology (relevant boarded areas include neuropsychology, geropsychology, and forensics), although most individuals who do geriatric assessments are not boarded.

Perhaps the most critical question is to *ascertain how much experience the professional has in the assessment of capacity of older adults*, or of clients with the type of presenting problem at hand.

When approaching the client's regular physician to request an evaluation, it is also useful to ask how long the physician has known the client. Armed with this information the lawyer will not only be in a better position to make a judgment about whether the individual is an "appropriate diagnostician," but also to convey in advance to the client what to expect as part of the evaluation.

Ideally, lawyers who have a large geriatric clientele will be able to recommend clinicians with whom they have had positive prior experience. Lawyers lacking those prior connections may wish to investigate resources through the local aging network. A good starting point is the local Area Agency on Aging for the county, city, or multi-county area in which the lawyer is located. Under the *Older Americans Act*, Area Agencies on Aging are responsible for planning and funding a wide range of services for older persons. They typically provide extensive information and referral services and may be able to identify health professionals with expertise in capacity assessment.

The American Psychiatric Association and American Psychological Association each have state and local affiliates. Sometimes these affiliates have referral lists based on area of expertise. State or local medical societies may be able to provide referral to geriatric medicine specialists or to physicians who identify themselves as having experience with older adults. University medical centers also may have geriatric or long-term care divisions with multi-disciplinary geriatric assessment teams.

For lawyers who see an increasing number of older adults in legal practice, it makes sense to develop referral resources in advance. In areas where there is a dearth of those with relevant specialty background, it might be possible to partner with a local health or mental health professional who is interested in gaining experience in this area.

Referral issues to consider:

1. **Use of consultation preliminary to referral;**
2. **Client consent for formal assessment; and**
3. **Lawyer communication with the assessor.**

The lawyer makes the final determination of capacity for the legal transaction

C. Elements of a Lawyer's Referral to a Clinician

Once a lawyer has identified good local clinical resources, the lawyer must consider the elements of an effective case referral. These elements are addressed below. The task of interpreting the assessment report is addressed in Chapter IX. Appendix 2 sets out a model letter requesting a client assessment.

Informal Consultation

A lawyer may consult a clinician either preliminary to or instead of making a client referral for a formal assessment. In such a consultation, the lawyer can outline client communications and reactions, as well as the legal transaction for which capacity is required. The lawyer can seek an informal opinion on the question of capacity—and on the question of whether a formal assessment is necessary. The clinician can raise questions the lawyer might have overlooked, allay or reframe the lawyer's concerns, and suggest strategies for enhancing client capacity.

A preliminary up-front consultation on capacity can bring a lot of "bang for the buck"–in some cases saving the lawyer and the client a great deal of time, money, and angst if it avoids an unnecessary formal assessment. Or it may provide reassurance that a formal assessment is indeed the right step, as well as an indication about what kind of assessment might be optimal.

As discussed further below, communication of capacity concerns to clients and families can sometimes be a difficult and unsettling process, which occasionally may lead abruptly to termination of the representation. Thus, an attorney needs to be well-prepared before taking such a formal step, and a private consultation may be one of the preparatory steps.

Client Consent for Informal Consultation

Does such a preliminary consultation require client consent? If the lawyer identifies the client in the consultation, the lawyer will breach Model Rule 1.6 mandating confidentiality by failing to seek consent. Moreover, the lawyer should aim to involve the client to the greatest extent possible in all aspects of the representation. However, the Comment to Model Rule 1.14 on clients with diminished capacity provides that "in appropriate circumstances, the lawyer may seek guidance from an appropriate diagnostician" in determining client capacity.[49] The comment does not address the question of consent for seeking such guidance.

On the question of disclosure of otherwise confidential information, the new Model Rule 1.14(c) provides that if the elements of Model Rule 1.14(b) are met (i.e., the lawyer reasonably believes the client has diminished capacity, is at risk of substantial harm, and unable to act adequately in his or her own interest), then the lawyer may "reveal information about the client, but only to the extent reasonably necessary to protect the client's interest." The obvious dilemma here is that the consultation may be needed prior to, and specifically, in order to determine whether the elements of Rule 1.14(b) are met—not after the lawyer has already come to that conclusion.

Asking about qualifications of clinicians

- **How long have you conducted such assessments?**
- **How many older adults have you assessed?**
- **What assessment approach and tools do you generally use?**
- **How many visits are usually required and of what duration?**
- **What is the likely cost of the assessment?**

One possible interpretation of the rule and comment is that, since consultation with an appropriate clinician is a very minimal protective action, the threshold for meeting the trigger criteria in Rule 1.14(b) is correspondingly low, thereby justifying very limited disclosure of otherwise confidential information. Unfortunately, authoritative resolution of the question is lacking.

The lawyer needs to use good judgment and limit information revealed to what is absolutely necessary to assist with a determination of capacity. Whenever possible, the lawyer should seek to consult the assessor informally without identifying the client. In that case, the question of consent does not arise. The consultation is simply professional advice to the lawyer.

Payment for Informal Consultation

What about payment? If the client is identified in the consultation and has given consent, the lawyer then can bill the client for the consultation, as well as for the time spent by the lawyer in speaking with the assessor. The lawyer should establish in advance the assessor fee for such consultations. However, if the client is not identified, the consultation is really a service for the lawyer, paid for by the lawyer.

Client Consent for Formal Assessment

Client consent for referral for a formal assessment involves some of the same ethical considerations as client consent for an informal consultation, outlined above. On the one hand, the lawyer must not breach the confidentiality that is the hallmark of the client-lawyer relationship, and on the other hand, the lawyer knows that an assessment of capacity is necessary to assure the validity of documents or to proceed with the task at hand. If the client seems unable to give consent, the lawyer could wait until the client is stabilized, and then explain the need for referral and seek consent, or at least the "assent" of the client.

Once the client has made contact with the clinical assessor, the assessor will need to ensure there is sufficient informed consent to conduct the evaluation.[50]

Finally, the clinician must get the client's consent to provide the test results to the lawyer under the requirements of the *Health Insurance Portability and Accountability Act* (HIPAA).[51] But beyond the ethical dictates, as a practical matter, there can be no referral unless the client at some level agrees to have an appointment with a clinician and to participate in the interview and the selected assessment tests.

How, then, does the lawyer broach the topic of a formal assessment with the client? Suggesting an assessment seems like an ultimate judgment by the lawyer–an authority figure in whom the client has placed trust. The client may interpret it as "My lawyer thinks I'm crazy... can't do things for myself ... have dementia ... am just an old woman." Indeed, "merely raising the issue of someone's competency [capacity] can be hurtful or damaging to them."[52] Moreover, the client may be intimidated by the very idea of a clinician asking questions or of having to take a test.

The referral is indeed trickier when the lawyer is not acting only to avoid later challenge, but because of genuine concern regarding the client's decision-making abilities, particularly in the context of undue influence. It is important to alert the client to the benefits as well as the risks of a capacity assessment. The clinician is duty bound to the same disclosure.

The best approach in such situations is a compassionate but honest and direct explanation such as:

> *Mrs. Jones, I am concerned about how you are doing. I am a little worried about your memory. To be sure that everything is okay for us to make this change to your will, and to make sure no one would contest it later, I would like you to meet with a clinician to do some formal assessment of your thinking. Hopefully, the testing will show us that everything is okay. If not, hopefully the testing will show us how to help you to meet your goals. The testing could come out either way, but I think it is a good idea to be sure. Is it okay if I set up an appointment for a specialist to talk with you and conduct the tests?*

Payment for Formal Assessment

Payment will also be a primary concern in making a referral for assessment by a clinician. If the assessment is related to a diagnosis of the client's condition or can be directly tied to his or her medical care, then the assessment may be billable under medical insurance or Medicare. However, when the assessment is strictly for a legal purpose and the client has given consent, the lawyer will need to disclose the likely cost of such assessment and confirm the client's payment obligation or other payment arrangement before proceeding.

Communicating with the Clinician

The care with which the lawyer crafts the referral request will bear on the usefulness of the results. Setting out the full information, the legal standard, and questions up front will be more likely to yield a well-tailored assessment report. Conversely, a poorly crafted referral without a clear statement of the purpose may get results that are simply not meaningful, not understandable, or just not on target.

The referral letter will be of greatest use if it clearly sets out the reason for the request, sufficient information about the client and the circumstances, and any legal standard of capacity involved. See an example of a referral letter in Appendix 2. As noted in the U.S. Department of Veterans Affairs *Practice*

Checklist of Lawyer Referral Letter Elements

1. **Client background: name, age, gender, residence, ethnicity, and primary language if not English.**
2. **Reason client contacted lawyer; date of contact; whether new or old client.**
3. **Purpose of referral: assessment of capacity to do what? Nature of the legal task to be performed, broken down as much as possible into its elemental components.**
4. **Relevant legal standard for capacity to perform the task in question.**
5. **Medical and functional information known: medical history, treating physicians, current known disabilities; any mental health factors involved; lawyer's observations of client functioning, need for accommodations.**
6. **Living situation; family make-up and contacts; social network.**
7. **Environmental/social factors that the lawyer believes may affect capacity.**
8. **Client's values and preference to the extent known; client's perception of problem.**
9. **Whether a phone consultation is wanted prior to the written report.**

Guidelines for Psychologists:

> There is always a specific reason why the psychologist is being consulted, and it is often not clearly stated. The psychologist must also understand the circumstances under which the person is allegedly unable to function under legal standards for competency. What specific areas of skill and function are at issue? In what circumstances and places? What other resources does the patient have to assist him/her in this matter? Why is the question being asked now? Was there a critical incident? Are there any major changes (e.g., surgery, relocation) which have had or might have a significant impact on this individual's ability to make decisions?[99]

It is important for the lawyer to communicate with the clinician orally, as well as in writing, to make sure the assessor understands the purpose for the referral and the elements outlined in the referral letter, as noted in the checklist on this page. The aim is to ensure a complete and well-targeted assessment that is worth the money spent. Having to fill in gaps or ambiguities afterwards is both costly and an inefficient use of everyone's time.

IX. Understanding and Using the Capacity Assessment Report

As the number of capacity assessments increases significantly over the next decades due to demographic changes, lawyers will become increasingly familiar with interpreting and using clinical assessments. Along with this, clinicians are developing practice standards and guidelines for such reports. This chapter aims to guide attorneys in the basic features and uses of a capacity assessment report.

The following description of a capacity assessment is drawn from a typical psychological or neuropsychological report, although the length of the report and elements included vary from practitioner to practitioner.

The term "patient" is used in this chapter since the capacity evaluation with a clinical examiner is a clinically oriented application despite its ultimate application in a legal setting. Examples of capacity evaluation reports are provided in Appendix 2.

A. Understanding the Elements of the Capacity Report

1. Demographic Information

The report should provide basic information concerning the age, race, gender, education, marital status, and vocational status of the patient. Such basic information provides a general context for the report's findings and conclusions.

2. Legal Background and Referral

A brief description of the legal matter or issues underlying the capacity issue should be referenced early in the report. This normally would include the referral source, the specific referral question(s) presented, and the elements of capacity at issue.

3. History of Present Illness

Frequently there are issues of medical and specifically neurologic and psychiatric illness that may be associated with the alleged diminished capacity of an individual. This medical history needs to be presented early in the report. Interview information obtained from the patient and collateral sources is an important part of this section.

Note: Reports of capacity assessment naturally differ somewhat depending on the professional discipline and to some extent the style of the clinician.

4. Psychosocial History

The report also concisely should reference relevant aspects of the patient's psychosocial history: family history; personal and family medical history; personal and family psychiatric history; social history; and work history.

5. Informed Consent

This section will document how the examiner described the purpose of the evaluation, and the patient's understanding of the evaluation and its risk and benefits, as well as the patient's consent to participate in the evaluation.

6. Behavioral Observations

Behaviors demonstrated by the patient during the course of the evaluation are often important pieces of capacity evidence and need to be set forth in the report. These can include the patient's appearance and presentation, speech and communication abilities, mood and range of emotional expression, insight and judgment, sense of humor, and test taking approach. Indications of

Common Elements of a Clinical Evaluation Report

Element	Summary
1. Demographic Information	Age, race, gender, education, etc.
2. Legal Background and Referral	Legal issue at hand, referral question
3. History of Present Illness	Medical history, current symptoms, etc.
4. Psychosocial History	Occupation, current living situation, family history of psychiatric and medical illness, etc.
5. Informed Consent	Statement of client's consent to the evaluation
6. Behavioral Observations	Appearance, speech, mood, etc.
7. Tests Administered	List of tests given
8. Validity Statement	Opinion of extent to which test results are valid
9. Summary of Testing Results	Test scores, standard scores, performance ranges as compared to age-matched normative data
10. Impression	Diagnosis; Clinical interpretation of test results; Clinical interpretation of psycho-legal capacities
11. Recommendations	If appropriate, statements of recommended clinical action (e.g., treatment to help symptoms)

neurologic or psychiatric illness should be noted, such as short-term memory loss (in interview); inability to follow task directions; confusion; perseverative behaviors or answering (i.e., excess repetition of a particular response, such as a word, phrase, or gesture); paranoid or delusional thinking; hallucinatory events; or the flat affect and morbid ideation characteristic of depression.

7. Tests Administered

A listing of the full range of tests administered should be included in the report. This would include tests that the patient discontinued or was unable to complete. There are many different psychological tests available that can be incorporated into a capacity evaluation. These are summarized in Appendix 1. However, in general, tests should cover the following general areas: (1) cognitive abilities; (2) personality and emotional functioning; and (3) relevant functional abilities. The functional category takes on particular significance in a capacity evaluation, as it will include (if available) measures of the specific capacities at issue in the legal case (e.g., medical decision-making capacity, financial capacity). However, as discussed further below, all three areas of testing are needed to comprise a comprehensive evaluation of the patient's capacity status.

When are objective tests indicated? The use of objective or performance-based instruments will vary according to the discipline of the assessor and the impairment of the client. As a rule, psychologists are more prone to use objective tests and to use more of them than physicians. Overall, the more mild, subtle, and complex a client's presentation, the more useful objective tests are likely to be. In contrast, a client with clear and obvious incapacity, such as in late-stage Alzheimer's disease, is unlikely to need or even to be able to complete most objective tests for the purposes of a capacity evaluation. Further, the more likely it is that the findings of the report will be disputed, the more important it will be to use standardized tests as these are more defensible as representing objective findings versus subjective opinion.

8. Validity Statement

An essential part of any report is a brief statement by the examiner concerning the validity of both the cognitive and emotional/personality test findings. For example, "the patient gave appropriate effort during the testing, and test results are judged to be a reliable and valid indicator of the patient's level of functioning." The validity of test results can be altered by factors such as low effort, frank attempts to exaggerate deficits, or unstable medical status. In most cases of unstable medical status, the examiner should wait until the patient is medically stable, but this is not always possible when an immediate result is needed. The validity measures will assist in this formulation, but other test-taking behaviors and factors also need to be considered.

Exaggerated test-taking performance and sometimes outright malingering can emerge in a capacity evaluation, although most older adults will be motivated to perform at their best when the purpose is to confirm capacity for legal transactions they have initiated, as compared to personal injury and workmen's compensation settings. The validity statement focuses on effort and motivation as it influences test performance. The impact of other variables such as education, socio-economic background, and ethnicity is considered in the interpretation in the impression section.

9. Summary of Testing Results

A summary of the test results should be presented as part of the report, either in text or tabular form. Although textual description of test data is probably most common, a tabular format can be very effective as it can efficiently present the full range of data obtained (raw scores, subscale scores, percentile ranks), organized by cognitive, personality, and functional sections.

10. Diagnostic & Clinical Interpretation

This section of the report integrates all of the evaluation information into a set of clinical and capacity findings. This is a significant undertaking, as multiple sources and levels of information (from the medical record, the clinical interviews, behavioral observations, and the multiple types of tests administered) must be considered, weighed, and then translated into diagnostic findings and, separately, into clinical interpretation. For example, the clinician may state that the test results are consistent with dementia, and the patient is capable of making simple medical decisions but lacks the capacity to make complex medical and financial decisions. It is at this juncture that the value of retaining a clinician with experience in capacity evaluations will be underscored. An effective approach is to report the diagnostic impressions, cognitive, and personality impressions first, in a separate section, as prelude to clinical interpretation of the psycho-legal capacities.

The next section can detail the clinician's opinion of the client's psycho-legal capacities. This opinion reflects not merely a scoring and reporting of test results, but a process of clinical inquiry and interpretation. It is important to keep in mind that the cognitive and emotional/personality findings and diagnostic assignments will not be determinative, by themselves, of the capacity outcomes in a particular matter. The capacity outcomes depend primarily on the fit, as judged by the examiner, between the individual patient's current functional abilities and the demands of the capacity in question within the patient's life context.

Thus, as an example, a patient diagnosed with mild Alzheimer's disease and mild to moderate memory impairment may still be quite capable of consenting to medical treatment, if he or she demonstrates sufficient treatment consent abilities such as appreciation, reasoning, and understanding in discussing a medical intervention with a physician.

Finally, the clinical interpretation may include recommendations for enhancing capacity and supporting decision making. Such findings may also reference prognosis and follow-up. More on clinical interventions and re-evaluation is provided on the following pages.

B. Clinical Capacity Opinions Versus Legal Capacity Outcomes

Capacity opinions in a report often are presented in terms of the patient being capable, marginally capable, or incapable with respect to the particular capacity in question (e.g., testamentary capacity). These capacity findings are clinical opinions, which although highly relevant to the legal capacity question at issue, are also distinct. It is at this point that the distinction between "clinical capacity" and "legal capacity" is most apparent and relevant.

Capacity evaluations should not (but in some cases may) present capacity opinions as actual findings of legal capacity. Clinical findings are evidence which must then be adduced by the attorney to support, along with other evidentiary sources, his or her judgment concerning the legal capacity issue at hand, such as the ability to change a will. In guardianship, judges use capacity evaluations as one form of evidence (albeit highly relevant and probative) in arriving at their determination of the need for guardianship or conservatorship.

C. Using the Capacity Report

A capacity report, like other expert sources of evidence, is subject to multiple uses.

Follow-up with Examiner

Upon receiving a capacity evaluation, an attorney should allocate time to read and digest the report as thoroughly as possible. This will permit an informed follow-up with the examiner to identify, for example, other issues needing attention or, on occasion, factual inaccuracies needing correction. Also, the attorney may need to clarify the meaning of technical language or abbreviations used in the report.

Use of the Report as Evidence

The attorney may treat the report as informational and advisory, or as a formal assessment that could be used as evidence in a judicial setting. If the examiner is not to be designated as an expert witness in a hearing or trial, the report will in most instances not be subject to discovery, and can remain advisory in nature, as part of the attorney's client case file.

However, the application of client-lawyer privilege and doctor-patient privilege varies among the states and may not protect the report from discovery. In some cases, the attorney has sought a capacity evaluation and report specifically for purposes of inclusion in the record to substantiate or refute the client's ability concerning a legal transaction, and, in the case of guardianship, for presentation as evidence at the hearing.

Limited Guardianship and the Least Restrictive Alternative

In general, during a guardianship or conservatorship proceeding, the findings of a capacity report should be used to support an outcome consistent with the least restrictive alternative. Thus, where possible, the findings should be used to frame judicial orders of limited guardianship or conservatorship, reserving to the client rights and powers in all areas in which he or she still retains decisional abilities. Thus, with respect to a conservatorship order, if the capacity evaluation suggests preserved abilities regarding handling small amounts of money and a small checking account, these activities (cash transactions, limited checkbook management) should be retained by the client as part of the overall order. The report also may substantiate the client's capacity to execute a durable power of attorney or a health care directive that may preclude the need for guardianship.

Protective Actions Under Model Rule 1.14

In some instances, the findings of the capacity evaluation may compel the attorney to take protective action with respect to an already existing client and his or her assets. Model Rule 1.14 requires that in situations of diminished capacity, the attorney take "reasonably necessary protective action." The presence of a sound capacity evaluation and report will likely make the attorney more comfortable in taking such actions, if indicated.

The Comment to Model Rule 1.14 provides the following examples of protective action and guiding principles:

> Such measures could include: consulting with family members, using a reconsideration period to permit clarification or improvement of circumstances, using voluntary surrogate decision-making tools such as durable powers of attorney, or consulting with support groups, professional services, adult protective agencies, or other individuals or entities that have the ability to protect the client. In taking any protective action, the lawyer should be guided by such factors as the wishes and values of the client to the extent known, the client's best interests and the goals of intruding into the client's decision-making autonomy to the least extent feasible, maximizing client capacities, and respecting the client's family and social connections.[100]

Clinical Interventions and Supports

There are many situations that are not adversarial, in which the attorney, client, and family are all seeking to serve the client's interests and to maximize capacity and autonomy. One important result of a capacity assessment may be specific recommendations for clinical interventions that may be recommended by the lawyer and pursued by the client and family to improve or stabilize the client's functioning. These are what is meant by supported decision-making strategies. For example, in the case of the older client who has become delusional in the context of a hearing impairment, isolation, and anxiety, clinical interventions to address all three (hearing aids, more social contact, anti-anxiety medication) may very well reduce or eliminate delusions and restore the individual's capacity. In other situations, more frequent oversight and assistance with nutrition and medication may increase the client's lucidity. Afterwards, the legal transaction may be appropriately pursued.

Re-Evaluation Over Time

Capacity status can fluctuate over time and in some instances a capacity that was initially lost (e.g., as a result of a head injury, transient acute psychosis, severe depression that later remits with treatment) will be recovered. In situations of intermittent or evolving capacity status, the value or need for a subsequent capacity evaluation should be considered.

For example, a client assessed as lacking capacity due to psychotic thinking that is secondary to severe depression may be re-evaluated for capacity after treatment for the depression. Similarly, a client assessed as lacking capacity due to confusion secondary to a urinary tract infection may similarly be re-evaluated.

Appendix 1: Brief Guide to Psychological and Neuropsychological Instruments

For the purpose of this appendix, psychological tests are described in four categories: (a) tests used to evaluate and document symptoms of cognitive impairment; (b) tests used to rate the type and severity of emotional or personality disorders; (c) tests used to detect unusual response styles, or the validity of test taking; (d) tests used to evaluate specific functional capacities or abilities. A brief guide to cognitive screening instruments is provided at the end of this appendix.

This listing is not meant as an exhaustive or definitive list but provides an overview of some of the more commonly assessed domains and tests. The number of tests can be somewhat overwhelming; added to this is that evaluators may refer to tests by shortened names or abbreviations. Data collected from an evaluation can aid in designing ways to support an older client's functioning and engagement in various capacities. For more information on specific tests, please refer to the reference books and resources noted at the end of this chapter.

A. Tests for Evaluating Cognitive Impairment

A comprehensive psychological or neuropsychological evaluation would typically assess the domains of appearance, level of consciousness, motor activity, mood, attention, learning and memory, language, executive functioning, visual-spatial or constructional ability, and verbal reasoning. Some of these areas are assessed through observation of the client's presentation and communication during a clinical interview. Other areas can be assessed through standardized, norm-referenced tests. Importantly, because of the complexity with how the brain is organized and works, several of these cognitive abilities are typically needed to complete any one of these instruments.

1. Appearance, Orientation, and Motor Activity

Definition: Although typically assessed through observation, not testing, an important part of a comprehensive evaluation is examination of appearance, hygiene and grooming, weight, motor activity (active, agitated, slowed), and orientation to who they are, where they are, time, and current events.

2. Level of Consciousness

Definition: Although also typically assessed through observation, not testing, the evaluator will observe the degree of alertness and general mental confusion, rating the client as alert, lethargic, or stupor. Additional assessment with basic measures of attention may be necessary.

3. Attention / Working Memory / Processing Speed

Definition: Several terms may be used by an examiner including attention, working memory, processing speed, concentration, and complex attention. These cover similar abilities but can be separated out as various types of attention-related abilities. They concern the ability to attend to a stimulus, temporarily store information, be free from distraction, and/or the speed with which a client can complete a task.

- *Tests:*
    - Working Memory subtests from the Wechsler Adult Intelligence Scale – IV (WAIS-IV)
    - Digit Span Forward / Digit Span Backward from the Neuropsychological Assessment Battery (NAB)
    - Attention subtests from the Repeatable Battery for the Assessment of Neuropsychological Status Update (RBANS)
    - Visual Working Memory subtests from the Wechsler Memory Scale-IV (WMS-IV)
    - Attention subtests from the Dementia Rating Scale-2 (DRS-2)
    - Trails A from the Trail Making Test (TMT)

4. Learning and Memory

Definition: Memory assessment involves evaluation of the system by which individuals register, store, retain, and retrieve information in verbal and visual domains. Depending on the measure selected, information may be available on a client's ability to recall information immediately, after a short delay, and again after a longer delay in time. Recommendations may also be available as to what extent assistance helps a client learn new information, access information stored in their memory, or recognize previously presented material.

- *Tests:*
    - WMS-IV
    - California Verbal Learning Test, second or third edition (CVLT-II or CVLT-3)
    - Immediate and Delayed Memory subtests from the RBANS
    - Rey Auditory Verbal Learning Test (RAVLT)
    - Hopkins Verbal Learning Test, Revised (HVLT-R)
    - Memory subtests from the NAB
    - Brief Visuospatial Memory Test, Revised (BVMT-R)

5. Language

Definition: Language includes a number of abilities such as spontaneous speech, the fluency of speech, repetition of speech, naming or word finding, reading, writing, and comprehension. The presence of aphasia (difficulty retrieving or expressing speech) and thought disordered speech is also noted.

- *Tests:*
    - Boston Naming Test-2 (BNT-2)
    - Boston Diagnostic Aphasia Examination-3 (BDAE-3)
    - Controlled Oral Word Association Test (COWAT, also commonly called the "FAS")
    - Animal Fluency
    - Language subtests from the RBANS
    - Token Test

6. Executive Function

Definition: The assessment of executive functions concerns a number of abilities such as planning, judgment, purposeful and effective action, volition, and mental flexibility. This area is often an extremely important aspect of assessing capacities, as it assists in evaluating a client's ability to adapt to new situations or tasks.

- *Tests:*
    - Clock Drawing Test (various versions exist)
    - Trails B from the TMT
    - Wisconsin Card Sorting Test (WCST)
    - Stroop Color Word Test (SCWT)
    - Delis-Kaplan Executive Function System (D-KEFS)
    - Category Test (Halstead-Reitan or Booklet)
    - Verbal Comprehension and Perceptual Reasoning subtests from the WAIS-IV
    - Executive Functions subtests from the NAB
    - COWAT
    - Frontal Assessment Battery (FAB)

7. Visual-Spatial and Visuo-Constructional Reasoning and Abilities

Definition: Visual spatial assessment involves evaluation of visual-spatial perception, problem solving, reasoning, and construction or motor performance.

- *Tests:*
    - Perceptual Reasoning subtests from the WAIS-IV
    - Clock Drawing Test
    - Rey-Osterrieth Complex Figure test (RCFT)
    - Hooper Visual Organization Test (HVOT)
    - Visuospatial / Constructional subtests from the RBANS
    - Judgment of Line Orientation (JLO)
    - Spatial subtests from the NAB
    - D-KEFS

8. Verbal Reasoning and Abilities

Definition: The assessment of verbal reasoning abilities involves evaluation of logical thinking, practical judgments, and comprehension of relationships. Related abilities are: fund of knowledge which is the extent of information known and retained, and calculation concerning arithmetic skills. There is clinical overlap between the executive functions and spatial reasoning mentioned above and verbal reasoning, but they can be differentiated via testing methods.

- *Tests:*
    - Verbal Reasoning subtests from the WAIS-IV
    - D-KEFS
    - Proverbs Tests
    - Math Computation subtest from the Wide Range Achievement Test-5 (WRAT5)
    - Mathematics subtests from the Woodcock-Johnson Tests of Achievement-IV (WJ IV ACH)

9. Motor Functions

Definition: Tests of motor function provide information about basic ability about praxis or motor skills in each hand, which are important for distinguishing observed deficits on tasks involving motor performance from primary (motor) or secondary (central nervous system) deficits.

- *Tests:*
    - Grooved Pegboard Test
    - Purdue Pegboard Test
    - Finger Tapping from the Halstead-Reitan Neuropsychological Battery (HRNB)
    - Grip Strength from the HRNB

B. Emotional and Personality Functioning

Tests of emotional and personality functioning can provide a more objective means to assess the range and severity of emotional and personal dysfunction.

1. Emotional Functioning

Definition: These scales assess the individual's degree of depressed or anxious mood, and associated symptoms such as insomnia, fatigue, low energy, low appetite, loss of interest or pleasure, irritability, feeling of helplessness, or suicidal ideation. Some scales will also assess the degree of hallucinations, delusions, and suspicious or hostile thought processes.

- *Tests:*
    - Geriatric Depression Scale (GDS, various versions)
    - Beck Depression Inventory-II (BDI-II)

  - Patient Health Questionnaire-9 (PHQ-9)
  - Cornell Scale for Depression in Dementia (CSDD)
  - Geriatric Anxiety Inventory (GAI)
  - Geriatric Anxiety Scale (GAS)
  - Beck Anxiety Inventory (BAI)
  - Rating Anxiety in Dementia Scale (RAID)
  - Brief Symptom Inventory-18 (BSI-18)
  - Symptom Checklist-90, Revised (SCL-90-R)

2. Personality

Definition: Personality inventories are occasionally used in capacity assessment to explore unusual ways of interacting with others and looking at reality that may be impacting sound decision-making. Projective personality inventories are relatively less structured and allow the patient open-ended responses. Objective tests in contrast typically provide a question and ask the patient to choose one answer (e.g., "yes" or "no").

- *Tests:*
  - Minnesota Multiphasic Personality Inventory, second or third edition (MMPI-2 or MMPI-3)
  - Minnesota Multiphasic Personality Inventory-2, Restructured Form (MMPI-2-RF)
  - Personality Assessment Inventory (PAI)
  - Million Clinical Multiaxial Inventory-IV (MCMI-IV)
  - Rorschach

C. Tests of Effort, Motivation, or Response Style

These measures, also referred to as performance validity tests, are structured in such a way to detect inconsistent or unlikely response patterns indicative of attempts to exaggerate cognitive problems. They serve as one type of evidence permitting the clinician to judge the validity of the overall cognitive testing. Generally, they detect test-taking response patterns that deviate from chance responding or from norms for established cognitively impaired clinical populations like Alzheimer's disease. If the tests are positive, they may indicate an intentional test-taking approach to exaggerate deficits. It remains a clinical judgment as to how to interpret the clinical meaning of test-taking bias/exaggeration. In some cases, they may reflect malingering for monetary secondary gain, whereas in other they may indicate a factitious disorder or sometimes a somatoform disorder. Tests of validity may be used when the examiner is concerned that the individual has a reason to gain from "faking bad" on the test, such as in disability claims. Older adults who are receiving capacity evaluations are most likely to be giving maximal effort to perform at their highest level in which case formal tests of validity are probably not indicated.

Definition: Validity tests are structured in such a way to detect inconsistent or unlikely response patterns indicative of attempts to exaggerate cognitive dysfunction. Many cognitive and psychological measures have embedded indicators of performance validity.

- *Tests*
  - Test of Memory Malingering (TOMM)
  - 21-Item Test
  - 15-Item Test
  - Forced Choice subtest of the CVLT-II or CVLT-3

D. Tests for Evaluating Specific Capacities or Abilities

When a capacity is specifically in question, a comprehensive evaluation would include direct assessment of the area in question. We include here instruments designed for clinical (not research) use. Many additional measures of capacity have been created since the first edition of this handbook, particularly for execution-related capacities (e.g., financial decision making, independent living). We include a more detailed description of the more commonly used instruments. Specific information on reliability and validity relevant to the Daubert standard of scientific admissibility can be found in the test manual or original research articles.

1. Adult Functional Adaptive Behavior Scale (AFABS)

Primary Reference: Pierce, P. S. (1989). *Adult functional adaptive behavior scale (AFABS): Manual of directions*. Togus, ME: Author.

Area(s) Assessed: Functional Abilities for Independent Living

Description: The Adult Functional Adaptive Behavior Scale (AFABS) was developed to assist in the assessment of ADL and IADL functions in the elderly to evaluate their capacity for personal responsibility and the matching of a client to a placement setting. The AFABS consists of 14 items. Six items rate ADLs: eating, ambulation, toileting, dressing, grooming, and managing (keeping clean) personal area. Two items tap IADLs: managing money and managing health needs. Six items tap cognitive and social functioning: socialization, environmental orientation (ranging from able to location room up through able to travel independently in the community), reality orientation (aware of person, place, time, and current events), receptive speech communication, expressive communication, and memory. Items are rated on four levels: 0.0 representing a lack of the capacity, 0.5 representing some capacity with assistance, 1.0 representing some capacity without assistance, and 1.5 representing independent functioning in that area. Individual scores are summed to receive a total score in adaptive functioning. The AFABS assesses adaptive functioning through interviewing an informant well-acquainted with the functioning of the individual in question. The informant data is combined with the examiner's observation of an interaction with the client to arrive at final ratings. The AFABS is designed for relatively easy and brief administration (approximately 15 minutes). The author recommends it be administered only by professionals experienced in psychological and functional assessment, specifically a psychologist, occupational therapist, or psychometrician, although research with the AFABS has also utilized psychiatric nurses and social workers trained in its administration.

2. Aid to Capacity Evaluation (ACE)

Primary Reference: Etchells, E., Darzins, P., Silberfeld, M., Singer, P. A., McKenny, J., Naglie, G., Katz, M., Molloy, D. W., & Strang, D. (1999). Assessment of patient capacity to consent to treatment. *Journal of General Internal Medicine, 14,* 27-34.

Area(s) Assessed: Medical Decision Making

Description: The ACE is a semi-structured assessment interview that addresses seven facets of capacity for an actual medical decision: the ability to understand (a) the medical problem; (b) the treatment; (c) the alternatives to treatment; (d) the option of refusing treatment; (e) the ability to perceive consequences of accepting treatment; (f) refusing treatment; and (g) the ability to make a decision not substantially based on hallucinations, delusions, or depression. These reflect legal standards in Ontario, Canada, but also correspond to U.S. legal standards. Questions in the areas a-d assess the decisional ability of understanding. Questions in areas e and f appear to tap reasoning, and in area g diminished appreciation based on patently false beliefs (e.g., "Do you think we are trying to harm you?").

3. **Assessment of Capacity to Consent to Treatment (ACCT)**

Primary Reference: Moye, J., Karel, M. J., Edelstein, B., Hicken, B., Armesto, J. C., & Gurrera, R. J. (2007). Assessment of capacity to content to treatment. *Clinical Gerontologist, 31,* 37-66.

Area(s) Assessed: Medical Decision Making

Description: The Assessment of Capacity to Consent to Treatment (ACCT) is a standardized measure of medical decision-making ability. Originally designed for research use, the manual indicates it can be adapted for clinical use. The clinician begins with an interview about the client's values, preferences, relationships, quality of life, and their approach to making medical decisions (such as who they may typically include and to what extent). The clinician uses a semi-structured interview to discuss a current health situation, or, alternatively, if there is no current health decision to be made, three vignettes are available for use. In each approach, the client is questioned regarding their understanding, appreciation, reasoning, and communication a choice. Scoring guidance is provided. During administration, the client is presented with bulleted lists of information in order to reduce the demand on memory. The manual provides extensive information on the creation, reliability, and validity of the ACCT.

4. **Assessment of Capacity for Everyday Decision-Making (ACED)**

Primary Reference: Lai, J. M., Gill, T. M., Cooney, L. M., Bradley, E. H., Hawkins, K. A., & Karlawish, J. H. (2008). Everyday decision-making ability in older persons with cognitive impairment. *American Journal of Geriatric Psychiatry, 16,* 693-696.

Area(s) Assessed: Decision Making for Independent Living

Description: The Assessment of Capacity for Everyday Decision-Making (ACED) is a semi-structured interview assessing the client's capacity to make decisions about solving functional problems, an ability the authors' term everyday decision-making. The ACED assesses understanding, appreciation, reasoning, and expressing a choice across several different functional deficits, such as managing medications or preparing meals. Importantly, the examiner collects information about the client's level of functioning prior to the evaluation, so that the ACED interview is tailored to each client's unique areas of functional concern. The measure can be completed in about 15 to 20 minutes. The ACED demonstrated good reliability and additional psychometric data is available in the primary reference. The ACED is useful in evaluating patients nearing a discharge from the hospital or when there are concerns about self-neglect. A shorter version is also available (The Short Portable Assessment of Capacity for Everyday Decision-Making).

5. **Capacity Assessment Tool (CAT)**

Primary Reference: Carney, M. T., Neugroschl, J., Morrison, R. S., Marin, D., & Siu A. L. (2001). The development and piloting of a capacity assessment tool. *Journal of Clinical Ethics, 12*, 17-23.

Area(s) Assessed: Medical Decision Making

Description: The CAT proposes to evaluate capacity based on six abilities: communication, understanding choices, comprehension of risks and benefits, insight, decision/choice process, and judgment. It uses a structured interview format to assess capacity to choose between two options in an actual treatment situation; as such, it does not use a hypothetical vignette.

6. Capacity to Consent to Treatment Interview (CCTI)

Primary Reference: Marson, D. C., Ingram, K. K., Cody, H. A., & Harrell, L. E. (1995). Assessing the competency of patients with Alzheimer's disease under different legal standards: A prototype instrument. *Archives of Neurology, 52,* 949-954.

Area(s) Assessed: Medical Decision Making

Description: The CCTI is based on two clinical vignettes; a neoplasm condition and a cardiac condition. Information about each condition and related treatment alternatives is presented at a fifth to sixth grade reading level with low syntactic complexity. Vignettes are presented orally and in writing; participants are then presented questions to assess their decisional abilities in terms of understanding, appreciation, reasoning, and expression of choice.

7. Competency Interview Schedule (CIS)

Primary Reference: Bean, G., Nishisato, S., Rector, N. A., & Glancy, G. (1996). The assessment of competence to make a treatment decision: An empirical approach. *The Canadian Journal of Psychiatry, 41,* 85-92.

Area(s) Assessed: Medical Decision Making

Description: The CIS is a 15-item interview designed to assess consent capacity for electro-convulsive therapy (ECT). Patients referred for ECT receive information about their diagnosis and treatment alternatives by the threating clinician, and the CIS then assesses decisional abilities based on responses to the 15 items.

8. Decision Assessment Measure

Primary Reference: Wong, J. G., Clare, I. C. H., Holland, A. J., Watson, P. C., & Gunn, M. (2000). The capacity of people with a 'mental disability' to make a health care decision. *Psychological Medicine, 30,* 295-306.

Area(s) Assessed: Medical Decision Making

Description: Wong et al., working in England, developed a measure that references incapacity criteria in England and Wales (understanding, reasoning, and communicating a choice), based on methodology by Grisso et al. (1995). Their instrument also assesses the ability to retain material because it is one of the legal standards for capacity in England and Wales (though not in the United States). A standardized vignette regarding blood drawing is used to assess paraphrased recall, recognition, and non-verbal demonstration of understanding (pointing to the correct information on a sheet with both correct information and distractor/incorrect information).

9. Decision-Making Instrument for Guardianship (DIG)

Primary Reference: Anderer, S. J. (1997). *Developing an instrument to evaluate the capacity of elderly persons to make personal care and financial decisions*. Unpublished doctoral dissertation, Allegheny University of Health Sciences.

Area(s) Assessed: Self-care, Home care, Financial

Description: The Decision-Making Instrument for Guardianship (DIG) was developed to evaluate the abilities of individuals to make decisions in everyday situations often the subject of guardianship proceedings. The instrument consists of eight vignettes describing situations involving problems in eight areas: hygiene, nutrition, health care, residence, property acquisition, routine money management in property acquisition, major expenses in property acquisition, and property disposition. Examinees are read a brief vignette describing these situations in the second person. Detailed scoring criteria are used to assign points for aspects of problem solving, including defining the problem, generating alternatives, consequential thinking, and complex/comparative thinking. The DIG is carefully standardized. Standard instructions, vignettes, questions, and prompts are provided in the manual. In addition, detailed scoring criteria are provided. Sheets with simplified lists of salient points of each vignette, provided in large type are provided, help to standardize vignette administration, and emphasize the assessment of problem solving and not reading comprehension or memory. Vignettes are kept simple, easy to understand, and brief.

10. Direct Assessment of Functional Status-Revised (DAFS-R)

Primary Reference: McDougall, G. J., Becker, H., Vaughan, P. W., Acee, T. W., & Delville, C. L. (2010). The revised direct assessment of functional status for independent older adults. *The Gerontologist, 50,* 363-370.

Area(s) Assessed: Functional Abilities for Independent Living

Description: The Direct Assessment of Functional Status-Revised (DAFS-R) is a revision of the original measure created by Loewenstein et al. (1989). This revised version aims to address concerns that the original measure may not have been sensitive enough to detect subtle changes in functional abilities. Several items were removed or altered. Research supports the validity and reliability of the revised version. The DAFS-R contains 55 items across the following domains: communication skills, financial skills, shopping skills, and medication skills. Clients are asked to demonstrate their abilities across these skills during the examination, rather than relying on self-report of abilities. For example, a client is asked to identify several aspects of a medication, such name, special instructions, and prescribing doctor, by looking at a medication bottle provided.

11. Financial Capacity Instrument (FCI-9)

Primary Reference: Marson, D. C., Sawrie, S. M., Snyder, S., McInturff, B., Boothe, T. S., Aldridge, T., Chatterjee, A., & Harrell, L. E. (2000). Assessing financial capacity in patients with Alzheimer's disease: A conceptual model and prototypical instrument. *Archives of Neurology, 57,* 877-884.

Area(s) Assessed: Financial Skills and Decision Making

Description: The Financial capacity Instrument (FCI) was designed to assess everyday financial activities and abilities. The instrument assesses six domains of financial activity: basic monetary skills, financial conceptual knowledge, cash transactions, checkbook management, bank statement management, and financial judgment. The FCI is reported to require between 30 minutes to 50 minutes to administer, depending on the cognitive level of the examinee. The FCI uses an explicit protocol for administration and scoring.

12. Financial Decision Tracker (FDT)

Primary Reference: Lichtenberg, P. A., Ficker, L., Rahman-Filipiak, A., Tatro, R., Farrell, C., Speir, J. J., Mall, S. J., Simasko, P., Collens, H. H., & Jackman, J. D. (2016). The Lichtenberg financial decision screening scale: A new tool for assessing financial decision making and preventing financial exploitation. *Journal of Elder Abuse & Neglect, 28,* 134-151.

Area(s) Assessed: Financial Decision Making

Description: The Financial Decision Tracker (FDT) was formerly known as the Lichtenberg Financial Decision Screening Scale. Based on a conceptual model of financial decision making, this screening measure consists of 10 questions designed to assess intellectual factors of choice, rationale, understanding, and appreciation. It takes approximately 10 minutes to administer. The FDT uses a specific financial decision, rather than a vignette, to evaluate judgment and vulnerability. Importantly, the client's financial decision is considered along with their values. This brief measure is designed to be administered by a variety of clinical and non-clinical professionals working with older adults. Online training is required for use and proper administration.

13. Financial Vulnerability Assessment (FVA)

Primary Reference: Lichtenberg, P. A., Stoltman, J., Ficker, L. J., Iris, M., & Mast, B. (2015). A person-centered approach to financial capacity assessment: Preliminary development of a new rating scale. *Clinical Gerontologist, 38,* 49-67.

Area(s) Assessed: Financial Decision Making

Description: The Financial Vulnerability Assessment (FVA) was formerly known as the Lichtenberg Financial Decision Rating Scale. Based on a conceptual model of financial decision making, the FVA is an in-depth structured interview for trained clinicians. Across 34 questions, the FVA assesses intellectual and contextual factors related to financial decision making. In this model, intellectual factors include choice, rationale, understanding, and appreciation. Conceptual factors include financial situational awareness, psychological vulnerability, and susceptibility. Online training is required for use and proper administration.

14. Hopemont Capacity Assessment Interview (HCAI)

Primary Reference: Edelstein, B. (1999). *Hopemont capacity assessment interview: Manual and scoring guide.* Morgantown, WV: Author.

Area(s) Assessed: Financial, Medical Decision Making

Description: The Hopemont Capacity Assessment Interview (HCAI) is a semi-structured interview in two sections. The first section is for assessing capacity to make medical decisions. The second section is for assessing capacity to make financial decisions and will be discussed here. In the interview the examinee is first presented with concepts of choice, cost, and benefits and these concepts are reviewed with the examinee through questions and answers. The examinee is then presented medical or financial scenarios. For each scenario, the individual is asked basic questions about what he or she has heard, and then are asked to explain costs and benefits, to make a choice, and to explain the reasoning behind that choice. The HCAI uses a semi-structured format. General instructions are provided. Specific standardized introductions, scenarios, and follow-up questions are on the rating form.

15. Hopkins Competency Assessment Test (HCAT)

Primary Reference: Janofsky, J. S., McCarthy, M., & Folstein, M. F. (1992). The Hopkins competency assessment test: A brief method for evaluating patients' capacity to give informed consent. *Hospital and Community Psychiatry, 43,* 132-136.

Area(s) Assessed: Informed Consent, Medical Decision Making, and Writing Advance Directives

Description: The Hopkins Competency Assessment Test (HCAT) is a brief screening tool for assessing a client's capacity to make treatment decisions and prepare advance directives. The measure is six items, with scores ranging from zero to ten. Clients are provided with a short essay on informed consent and durable power of attorneys and afterwards are asked to complete a questionnaire about what they read. These may be read aloud if needed. The questionnaire consists of true/false and sentence completion. Scores on the questionnaire correlated with a psychiatrist's blinded judgment of the patient's capacity.

16. Independent Living Scales (ILS)

Primary Reference: Loeb, P.A. (1996). *Independent Living Scales.* San Antonio, TX: Psychological Corporation.

Area(s) Assessed: Care of home, Health care, Financial

Description: The Independent Living Scales (ILS) is an individually administered instrument developed to assess abilities of the elderly associated with caring for oneself and/or for one's property. The early version of the ILS was called the Community Competence Scale (CCS). The CCS was constructed specifically to be consistent with legal definitions, objectives, and uses, in order to enhance its value for expert testimony about capacities of the elderly in legal guardianship cases. The ILS consists of 70 items in five subscales: Memory/Orientation, Managing Money, Managing Home and Transportation, Health and Safety, and Social Adjustment. The five subscales may be summed to obtain an overall score, which is meant to reflect the individual's capacity to function independently overall. Two factors may be derived from items across the five subscales: Problem Solving and Performance/Information. The ILS has extensive information on norms, reliability, and validity.

17. MacArthur Competence Assessment Tool – Treatment (MacCAT-T)

Primary Reference: Grisso, T., & Appelbaum, P. S. (1998). *Assessing competence to consent to treatment: A guide for physicians and other health professionals.* New York, NY: Oxford.

Area(s) Assessed: Medical Decision Making

Description: The MacCAT-T utilizes a semi-structured interview to guide the clinician through an assessment of the capacity to make an actual treatment decision. It does not use a standardized vignette. Patients receive information about their condition, including the name of the disorder, its features and course, then are asked to "Please describe to me your understanding of what I just said." Incorrect or omitted information is cued with a prompt (e.g., "What is the condition called?"), and if still incorrect or omitted, presented again. A similar disclosure occurs for the treatments, including the risks and benefits of each treatment alternative. Next, patients are asked if they have any reason to doubt the information and to describe that. They are then asked to express a choice and to answer several questions that explicate their reasoning process, including comparative and consequential reasoning and logical consistency. The MacCAT-T was based on three pre-cursor instruments: Perception of Disorder (POD), Thinking Rationally About Treatment (TRAT), and the Understanding Treatment Disclosures (UTD).

18. Making and Executing Decisions for Safe and Independent Living (MED-SAIL)

Primary Reference: Mills, W. L., Regev, T., Kunik, M. E., Wilson, N. L., Moye, J., McCullough, L. B., & Naik, A. D. (2014). Making and executing decisions for safe and independent living: Development and validation of a brief screening tool. *American Journal of Geriatric Psychiatry, 22,* 285-293.

Area(s) Assessed: Decision Making for Independent Living

Description: The Making and Executing Decisions for Safe and Independent Living (MED-SAIL) is a brief screening tool designed to identify clients with impaired capacity to live in the community. Several hypothetical community living scenarios are available, such running out of medications or locking yourself out of your home. After review of the client's situation, two to three scenarios are selected for administration. Interviewing allows for prompts to gain a better sense of decision making ("what would you do if…."). The MED-SAIL assesses understanding, appreciation, expressing a choice, problem solving, comparative reasoning, and generating consequences. After a review of the scores, the examiner assigns a rating of no, partial, or full capacity. This measure can be used by a variety of healthcare and social service professionals in identifying if a referral for a formal evaluation is necessary.

19. Multidimensional Functional Assessment Questionnaire (MFAQ)

Primary Reference: Fillenbaum, G. G., & Smyer, M. A. (1981). The development, validity, and reliability of the OARS multidimensional functional assessment questionnaire. *Journal of Gerontology: Psychological Sciences, 36,* 428-434.

Area(s) Assessed: Functional Abilities for Independent Living

Description: The Multidimensional Functional Assessment Questionnaire (MFAQ) was developed to provide a reliable and valid method for characterizing elderly individuals and for describing elderly populations. The MFAQ supersedes the nearly identical Community Survey Questionnaire (CSQ, a predecessor which also was developed by the Duke Center). Both instruments frequently have been called the OARS in reference to the program that developed the instrument throughout the 1970s. The MFAQ or the CSQ was already in use by well over 50 service centers, researchers, or practitioners nationally when the MFAQ was published (1978). Part A provides information in five areas of functioning, including activities of daily living. The Activities of Daily Living (ADL) dimension assesses 14 functions including both instrumental and physical ADLs. Instrumental ADLs listed include using the telephone, using transportation, shopping, preparing meals, doing housework, taking medicine, and handling money. Physical ADLs include eating, dressing oneself, care for one's own appearance, walking, getting in/out of bed, bathing, getting to the bathroom, and continence. Part B of the MFAQ assess the individual's utilization of services, that is, whether and to what extent the examinee has received assistance from various community programs, agencies, relatives, or friends, especially within the last six months. Questioning also includes the examinee's perceived need for the various services.

20. Philadelphia Geriatric Center Multilevel Assessment Inventory (MAI)

Primary Reference: Lawton, M. P., Moss, M., Fulcomer, M., & Kleban, M. H. (1982). A research and service oriented multilevel assessment instrument. *Journal of Gerontology: Psychological Sciences, 37,* 91-99.

Area(s) Assessed: Function Abilities for Independent Living

Description: The Philadelphia Geriatric Center Multilevel Assessment Inventory (MAI) was designed to assess characteristics of the elderly relevant for determining their needs for services and placement in residential settings. The MAI is a structured interview procedure that obtains descriptive information about an elderly respondent related to seven domains. Each of the domains (except one) is sampled by interview questions in two or more subclasses, which the authors call sub-indexes. The full-length MAI consists of 165 items, the middle-length MAI has 38 items, and the short-form has 24 items. The domains assessed are physical health, cognitive abilities, activities of daily living, use of time, personal adjustment, social interaction, and perceived environment. The MAI manual provides considerable structure for the process of the interview, sequence and content of questions, and scoring. It describes criteria as a 1 to 5 rating for each of the domains, but these criteria are not tied specifically to item scores. The manual discusses general considerations for interviewing elderly individuals and dealing with special problems of test administration with this population (e.g., dealing with limited hearing or vision).

21. Structured Interview for Competency Incompetency Assessment Testing and Ranking Inventory (SICIATRI)

Primary Reference: Tomoda, A., Yasumiya, R., Sumiyana, T., Tsukada, K., Hayakawa, T., Matsubara, K., Kitamura, F., & Kitamura T. (1997). Validity and reliability of the structured interview for competency incompetency assessment testing and ranking inventory. *Journal of Clinical Psychology, 53,* 443-450.

Area(s) Assessed: Medical Decision Making

Description: The Structured Interview for Competency Incompetency Assessment Testing and Ranking Inventory (SICIATRI) assesses ability to provide informed consent to treatment. The development of this instrument included Japanese medical and psychiatric inpatients, with the SICIATRI administered upon admission to the hospital. Across 12 items, patients are evaluated on their level of insight, desire to get better, understanding of their condition, as well as the risk, benefits, and alternatives to treatment and no treatment. After rating the items, the examiner classifies the patient's capacity into one of five categories, ranging from "completely incompetent" to "completely competent." The primary reference offers information on the validity and reliability.

22. Texas Functional Living Scale (TFLS)

Primary Reference: Cullum, C. M., Weiner, M. F., & Saine, K. C. (2009). *Texas functional living scale: Examiner's manual.* San Antonio, TX: NCS Pearson.

Area(s) Assessed: Functional Abilities for Independent Living

Description: The Texas Functional Living Scale (TFLS) was designed as a measure of skills necessary for independent functioning. Specifically, clients are asked to perform a range of activities related to instrumental activities of daily living, such as using a telephone and a calendar. Designed to be brief in nature, the TFLS is comprised of 24 items across four subscales: Time, Money and Calculation,

Communication, and Memory. Scores are available for each subscale and for the overall measure and allow the examiner to compare the client's performance to a nationally normative sample. A review of the client's performance and scores aids in considering placement and assistance needs. The TFLS has been correlated with many other measures in this Appendix. The manual provides evidence on validity, reliability, and use of the TFLS with different diagnostic groups.

E. Cognitive Screening

Cognitive screening tests are useful for giving a general level of overall cognitive impairment, but they are insensitive to deficits in single domains (i.e., they can give you a sense that the brain overall is not working as well as expected but cannot tell you specifically where and why). They may be used as an overall screening to determine whether additional testing is needed. They may also be used for individuals with more severe levels of impairment who cannot complete other tests. Importantly, a total score on any of these instruments may be attributed to several factors (neurocognitive impairment, fatigue, emotional state, medications, etc.). All screening instruments include the potential for false positives (misidentifying someone as having cognitive impairment when they do not, or at least to the extent that the test may suggest) and false negatives (failing to detect someone as having cognitive impairment when they actually do). Only someone trained in test administration should interpret the test and make inferences. Careful consideration is needed regarding influence of age, race and ethnicity, gender, educational attainment, and prior levels of functioning.

Mini Mental Status Examination (MMSE): The MMSE is a 30-point screening instrument that assesses orientation, immediate registration of three words, attention and calculation, short term recall of three words, language, and visual construction. The MMSE is widely used and has adequate reliability and validity. Various versions are available.

Montreal Cognitive Assessment (MoCA): The MoCA is a 30-point screening instrument that assesses attention and concentration, executive functions, memory, language, visuoconstructional skills, conceptual thinking, calculations, and orientation. This measure is also widely used and has adequate reliability and validity. Various versions are available.

St. Louis University Mental Status Examination (SLUMS): The SLUMS is a 30-point screening instrument that assesses orientation, calculations, language, memory, attention, and visuoconstructional skills. The SLUMS has adequate reliability and validity. Only one version is available for use. It is commonly used in the Department of Veterans Affairs medical centers.

Cognistat: This screening instrument, formally known as the Neurobehavioral Cognitive Status Exam, assesses level of consciousness, orientation, attention, language, constructional ability, memory, calculations, and executive functioning. It has adequate reliability and validity. Various versions are available.

Mini-Cog: The Mini-Cog is a screening instrument that assesses short term recall of three words and visuoconstructional abilities (drawing a clock). This is one of the shortest measures on this list, taking about 3 minutes to administer, and can be easily integrated into a healthcare setting. Various versions are available. More research is needed, but it is included here given the increasing frequency of use and promotion as a brief screen by the Alzheimer's Association.

The Seven Minute Screen (7MS): This screening instrument consists of four subtests: recall, verbal fluency, orientation, and clock drawing. It is adequate test-retest reliability and inter-rater reliability. As the name suggests, it is a briefer measure than others on this list and is useful in a primary care setting.

General Practitioner Assessment of Cognition (GPCOG): The GPCOG is a 9-point screening instrument assessing orientation to time, visuoconstructional skills (clock drawing), current events, and recall. This measure has adequate reliability and validity. Scores are reportedly not influenced by cultural and linguistic background of the client. Various language versions are available, including an additional form for interviewing an informant.

F. Suggested Test Reference Books / Resources

Carlson, J. E., Geisinger, K. E. & Jonson, J. L. (Eds.). (2020). *The twenty-first mental measurements yearbook*. Lincoln, NE: Buros Center for Testing.

Ghesquiere, A. R., McAfee, C., & Burnett, J. (2019). Measures of financial capacity: A review. *The Gerontologist, 59*, e109-e129.

Lezak, M. D., Howieson, D. B., Bigler, E. D., & Tranel, D. (2012). *Neuropsychological assessment* (5th ed.). New York, NY: Oxford University Press.

Lichtenberg, P. A. (Ed.). (2010). *Handbook of assessment in clinical gerontology* (2nd ed.). Burlington, MA: Academic Press.

Palmer, B. W., & Harmell, A. L. (2016). Assessment of healthcare decision-making capacity. *Archives of Clinical Neuropsychology, 31*, 530-540.

Tuokko, H. A., & Smart., C. M. (2018). *Neuropsychology of cognitive decline: A developmental approach to assessment and intervention*. New York, NY: Guilford.

Appendix 2: Case Example

Introduction to Case Example

The case example below involves a client for which there are more than mild concerns about capacity, and where the lawyer decides to seek a formal assessment. It provides an example of a thorough referral and good quality assessment report and describes how the lawyer used such reports to guide follow-up action. In this example, the formal assessment was written by a psychologist. As noted in the handbook, the style of the report received will vary depending on the discipline of the assessor.

Concerns about Mr. Patient's proposed Contract, Will, and Financial Management Abilities

A. Example of Attorney Model Referral Letter

RE: Referral of Mr. Patient for Mental Health Assessment

Dear____________________:

As we discussed by telephone, I am writing to make a referral of Mr. Patient for a neuropsychological assessment, with emphasis on his capacity: (1) to contract, (2) to make a will, and (3) to manage his business and financial affairs, as well as (4) his vulnerability to undue influence.

Background

I represented Mr. Patient and his now deceased wife several years ago in preparing their estate plan. Recently, Mr. Patient requested that I redraft a will for him and prepare a buy/sell agreement for him with respect to his company Happy Valley Construction, which he owns with his brother James. Mr. Patient is 76 years old, was born and raised in Columbus, Georgia. He lives alone in his home of 34 years, although he receives home care services every day. His wife of 40 years died in 2015. He has two married daughters and one disabled single son. His daughter, Mrs. Daughter, is the only one who lives close by. She regularly helps him with shopping, paying bills, cooking, and light housekeeping. She is also named as his agent on his general durable power of attorney for financial affairs. However, she has not yet assumed the role of acting as his agent or attorney-in-fact.

As a result of my preliminary information gathering of his business and personal financial circumstances, as well as direct observations of Mr. Patient, I recommended to him that he undergo this formal evaluation. He consented to the assessment, to have the results of the assessment released to me (release attached), and to pay the cost of the assessment. He should be billed directly by you. He has also consented to your contacting his daughter for additional background information.

Triggering Issue

Mr. Patient's daughter, Mrs. Daughter, called my office to make an appointment for her father to review a contract (a buy-sell agreement) that Mr. Patient's brother asked him to sign. She also said that her father wanted to discuss rewriting his will.

I met with Mr. Patient on x/xx/xx for part of the time in private and for part of the time with his daughter present. While he appeared well-groomed and dressed appropriately and was able to describe the purpose of his visit, he showed considerable difficulty understanding the contents of the contract that his brother asked him to sign. The buy-sell contract would give his brother a first option to acquire his interest in their closely-held family company (Happy Valley Construction) on very favorable terms. But it also goes a significant step further in vesting the entire company in his brother upon Mr. Patient's death and forgiving several unspecified loans made by Mr. Patient to the company. The daughter expressed concern that her uncle is taking advantage of her father's diminished health in urging him to sign such a one-sided agreement.

As to his will, he urgently wants to redo it, now that his wife has died (although her death is now several years passed). I had prepared his current will when his wife was still alive. Under his current will, his disabled son would receive half the estate in trust, while the two daughters would each get one-quarter of the estate. He states that he now wants everything to go equally to his three children, but he appears to be confused about the nature and extent of property in his estate and about the terms of his present will.

His daughter also reports high levels of forgetfulness, confusion, and poor judgments, especially around financial transactions. She is concerned that he is unable to handle neither his business nor personal financial affairs, and she currently does most of his personal bill paying for him.

Relevant Legal Standards

Contractual capacity. In this state, the test of whether party has sufficient mental capacity to execute a valid contract is whether he is possessed of sufficient mind and reason for a full and clear understanding of the nature and consequences of making the contract. A more complicated contract calls for a higher level of capacity than a simple one. While a buy-sell agreement is not unusually complex, the proposed agreement in this case goes well beyond the usual buy-sell terms and would, in effect, be a will substitute for a major part of his estate, as well as forgiving several loans (the number or amount of which I have not yet verified).

Testamentary capacity. In this state, the capacity to make a will is defined as requiring: (1) an understanding that a will is a disposition of property to take effect after death, (2) a general understanding of the property subject to the will, (3) a knowledge of the persons related to him by ties of blood and of affection who would be the usual beneficiaries of a will, and (4) an ability to conceive and express by words, written or spoken, or by signs, or by both, any intelligible scheme of disposition. It is possible for one to have testamentary capacity but not contractual capacity.

Legal incapacity to manage one's property. This is the standard used to determine the need for a court-appointed guardian in this state: a court may appoint a guardian for a person who is: (1) incapacitated by reason of mental illness, mental retardation, mental disability, physical illness or disability, chronic use of drugs or alcohol, detention by a foreign power, disappearance, or other cause; and (2) as a result of such condition, incapable of managing his or her estate, and (3) the appointment is necessary either because the property will be wasted or dissipated unless proper management is provided or because the property is needed for the support, care, or well-being of such person or those entitled to be supported by such person.

Undue influence. "Undue influence" is influence that amounts either to deception or to force and coercion which destroys free agency. It is recognized that lesser amount of influence may be necessary to dominate a mind that is impaired by age or disease. However, honest persuasion or argument does not constitute undue influence in the absence of fraud or duress when the individual in question has the mental capacity to choose between his original intention and the wishes of the other person.

Medical/Social/Functional Information

Mr. Patient reports that he is on medication for diabetes and heart problems. His daughter reports that he had by- pass surgery in 2003 and that he had surgery on his lungs in 2016. His personal physician is Dr. Medical, at (address and phone). My contacts with Mr. Patient go back 15 years, and he was always quite knowledgeable in business affairs, very caring of his family, and active. My own observations are that he is now clearly quite frail and variable in his level of understanding, alertness, and confusion. Only his daughter appears to have regular contact with him. She is very concerned about his welfare and very distrustful of her uncle. The uncle essentially runs the business alone now but maintains contact with Mr. Patient. Mr. Patient appears to have great trust in his brother.

In summary, I request an evaluation for the purposes described above. Please include the following in your assessment report if possible:

- Mental health diagnosis
- Tests conducted
- Analysis of test results
- Applicability to situation at hand
- Specific assessment of the ability of Mr. Patient to:
    - execute a contract (the buy-sell agreement described above)
    - make a will
    - manage his business and financial affairs
- Assessment of his vulnerability to undue influence
- Suggestions for improving his capacity or accommodating his deficiencies, if any.

I understand that the evaluation and report can be completed by x/xx/xx. If that time frame changes, please let me know. Please send your report to me at my Columbus office address. I appreciate your help with the case and look forward to working with you in the future.

Sincerely,

____

B. Example of Psychological Assessment Report

Name: Mr. Patient
Sex: Male
Race: White
Age: 76
DOB: x/xx/xxxx
MRN: xxxxxxx

Education: 6
Occupation: Real estate/construction business owner
Marital Status: Widowed
Handedness: Right
Date Seen: x/xx/xx
Date of Report: x/xx/xx

BACKGROUND INFORMATION. Mr. Patient was referred as an outpatient to the Neuropsychology Clinic by his attorney, Mr. Legal, Esq., for evaluation of the patient's cognitive and emotional status, and capacities to contract (execute a buy/sell agreement), manage his overall business and financial affairs, and make a will.

History of Present Illness: Mr. Patient reportedly has a 3- to 5-year history of memory problems, which reportedly developed insidiously and have gotten progressively worse over time. He reportedly has not been previously evaluated for these problems.

In interview, Mr. Patient stated that he does not have any problems with his memory. He also generally denied any other cognitive or functional problems. He stated that he does not have any help at home, but that his daughter comes by sometimes to help him pay bills or to bring him groceries. He denied problems with his driving. Regarding mood or personality changes, he reported that he is "doing fine" and denied any symptoms of depression or anxiety. Upon inquiry by the examiner, he expressed only a vague knowledge of a buy-sell agreement regarding his business that has reportedly been prepared by his brother.

Mr. Patient's daughter, Ms. Daughter, described a much more serious situation. Ms. Daughter said that her father has had memory problems for at least 5 years, and that his memory has become noticeably worse over the past 3 years. She said that she first noticed something was different when she left her accounting job in the family business in 2016 over some disagreements with her uncle James, who co-owns the business with her father. She said that her father did not seem to be taking up for her, which was uncharacteristic of him. She said that she later realized that her father was forgetting about these disagreements and his role in resolving them. Ms. Daughter reported that he currently asks the same question repeatedly, forgets conversations, and constantly misplaces items. She said that he has more trouble remembering people's names. She said that he has comprehension problems but pretends to understand people when they talk to him. She reported that when they go to restaurants, he gets lost on his way back from the restroom. She reported that he has not driven since July 2017. She said that just prior to that, he complained to her about getting lost while driving in a familiar area.

Regarding functional changes, Ms. Daughter reported that her father has no meaningful activities around the home. He has had full-time caregivers since July 2018. She noted that he still cannot remember their names. She reported that prior to these home health care arrangements, her father was not bathing and was wearing the same clothes every day. She reported that she has handled all of her father's bill paying since October 2017. She said that she also tries to supervise his business transactions. Ms. Daughter reported that her father co-owns an excavation business Happy Valley Construction, with his brother James. The business is located in Columbus, Georgia.

Mr. Patient reportedly has a separate business where he also buys, develops, and sells real estate. Ms. Daughter stated that her father has agreed on several occasions to consult her before signing any business documents, but then forgets to do this.

Ms. Daughter reported several poor business decisions her father has made recently. She said that in the past year he sold a piece of real estate for $10,000 that was worth $100,000. She also reported that he has made almost $500,000 in loans to the family business over the past 5 years, and that these loans have not been repaid. She reported that her father initially loaned $200,000 to Happy Valley in 2016, after his wife died, $90,000 of which went to his nephew, who also works for the company. She stated that there does not appear to be a note for the loan to his nephew. She reported that the remaining $300,000 was loaned out in early 2017.

Ms. Daughter also expressed concern about a proposed buy-sell agreement that was presented to her father by his brother while she was out of town. This agreement reportedly presents terms that are very favorable to the brother. It apparently states that if her father dies, the company will go to her uncle James and the money owed by the company to her father will be forgiven. She noted that in this buy/sell agreement, some property that belongs to her father is listed instead as company property. Upon learning of this agreement, Ms. Daughter encouraged her father to contact his attorney Mr. Legal to discuss this.

Finally, Ms. Daughter expressed concern about whether her father may have recently signed a new will. Although he has no recollection of signing a new will, she indicated that he had stated that his brother had recently mentioned the "need" for a new will.

Regarding mood or personality changes, Ms. Daughter reported that her father is more laid back and even indifferent. She said that he used to be very focused on and concerned about his business affairs, but now seems often indifferent to them. She denied symptoms of anxiety or depression but noted that he naps a lot during the day. She also stated that he always wants to eat because he forgets that he has already eaten.

Social/Academic/Occupational History: Mr. Patient reportedly was born and raised in Columbus, Georgia. He reported that he had 4 brothers and sisters. The patient's father was a farmer and iron smith. The patient was reportedly married for 40 years when his wife died in 2015. He reported that he has two daughters and one son with a disability. He currently lives alone.

Mr. Patient reportedly completed 6 years of education. He reportedly buys and sells real estate and co-owns an excavation business called Happy Valley Construction Company, Inc. Mr. Patient reportedly started the excavation business and then brought his brothers into the business at a later time.

Prior Medical History: Mr. Patient's medical history reportedly is significant for diabetes and history of blood clots. Surgical history reportedly includes four-way coronary artery bypass graft (2003) and partial lung resection (2016). The patient reportedly does not drink alcohol and does not smoke. There is reportedly no history of alcohol or other substance abuse.

Family medical history is reportedly positive for myocardial infarction in his brother, stomach cancer in his sister, skin cancer in his sister, and possible Alzheimer's disease (AD) in his mother.

Psychiatric History: Mr. Patient reportedly has no history of mental health treatment. As noted above, he reportedly has had no prior evaluations for his memory problems.

Medications: Coumadin, Exelon, Prevacid, Tenormin, ginkgo biloba, Ambien, Detrol, Claritin.

BEHAVIORAL OBSERVATIONS. Mr. Patient presented as a well-groomed, nicely dressed 76year-old White man. He was accompanied to the evaluation by his daughter, Ms. Daughter.

In interview, the patient's speech was fluent and reasonably goal-directed but lacked spontaneity. Responses were terse and impoverished. Comprehension appeared generally intact. Affect was mildly constricted, and mood was pleasant but irritable. Insight was judged to be very poor. There was no indication or report of formal hallucinations or delusions, or of a thought or perceptual disorder. There was no indication or report of suicidal ideation, plan, or intent.

During testing, Mr. Patient was alert and pleasant but would quickly become irritable and uncooperative with testing. He exhibited mild performance anxiety. He displayed task frustration by abandoning or avoiding tasks. He showed no response to encouragement from the psychometric technician. He displayed inability to complete some tasks due to comprehension problems. He made a few perseverative and intrusion errors. He required constant redirection to task. He showed a complete lack of test-taking strategies.

At one point, he refused to continue testing and started to leave, but was persuaded by his daughter to continue. Because of his reluctance to participate, and the examiner's concern that he would prematurely terminate the testing, only an abbreviated test battery could be administered. Nevertheless, sufficient information was obtained to respond fully to the referral questions. Overall, the patient appeared to put forth variable but acceptable effort during the testing. Much of his reluctance to participate related to tasks that he appeared unable to perform. Overall, the current test results are an accurate representation of Mr. Patient's current levels of cognitive and emotional functioning, and of his current financial abilities.

TESTS ADMINISTERED

Clinical Interview
California Verbal Learning Test - 3 (CVLT-3)
Dementia Rating Scale-2 (DRS-2)
Executive Clock Drawing Task (CLOX)
Financial Capacity Instrument-9 (FCI-9)
Geriatric Depression Scale (GDS)
Test of Practical Judgment (TOP-J)
Token Test
Trails A and B
WAB-R Auditory Verbal Comprehension
Wide Range Achievement Test-5 (Blue Word Reading subtest)

SUMMARY OF RESULTS

Please see attachment.

IMPRESSIONS AND SUMMARY

Neuropsychological Findings:

1. Probable dementia, currently moderate (DRS-2=89/144, CDR= 2.0).

The neuropsychological test results were consistent with probable moderate dementia. Evidence for this impression included severe impairment on a dementia screening instrument and impairments in high-load verbal learning, recall, and recognition memory (severe to profound), simple short-term verbal recall (severe), orientation to time (severe), orientation to place (severe), simple auditory comprehension (severe), reading abilities (moderate), visuospatial construction of a clock drawing (mild), simple visuomotor tracking (mild), propositional auditory comprehension (moderate), and spontaneous construction of a clock drawing (severe). The patient was unable to complete a measure of visuomotor tracking/set flexibility. In addition, the patient's daughter reported that he has had progressive memory and other cognitive problems for as long as five years.

Functional testing and interview data were also consistent with moderate dementia. Mr. Patient was severely impaired on a cognitive measure of everyday problem-solving abilities. On a functional measure of financial capacity, the patient showed intact performance only on simple tasks of naming coins/currency, coin/currency relationships, and single and multi-item grocery purchases. He demonstrated significant impairment on tests of counting coins/currency, understanding financial concepts, making change for a vending machine, tipping, conceptual understanding of a bank statement, use of a bank statement, detection of telephone fraud, conceptual understanding of bills, identifying and prioritizing bills, and knowledge of his personal financial assets and activities. In addition, the patient's daughter indicated that he has home health care aides around the clock. She reported that prior to these arrangements, the patient was not bathing and wore the same clothes every day. She said that he currently has no meaningful activities around the home.

As discussed above, due to the patient's reluctance to participate fully in the testing, only an abbreviated test battery was administered. Some cognitive domains were not assessed (e.g., expressive language, general intellectual abilities), and other domains were not assessed as comprehensively as they normally would be.

2. Possible Alzheimer's disease.

Mr. Patient's neurocognitive profile was consistent with possible AD. High-load verbal learning, recall, and recognition memory were moderately to severely impaired and he was unable to benefit from semantic or recognition cueing. He showed 0% recall after a short delay, which is consistent with the rapid decay of information over delay seen in AD. In addition, he had 0% short-term recall of verbal items from the memory subtest of the DRS-2. Mr. Patient demonstrated characteristic impairments on measures of executive function (simple visuomotor tracking, propositional auditory comprehension, and spontaneous construction of a clock drawing) and inability to complete a measure of visuomotor tracking/set flexibility.

Clinical course was consistent with AD. Mr. Patient's cognitive difficulties reportedly have been slowly progressive over the past 5 years. He also has a family history of possible AD.

In the examiner's judgment, it is highly probable that Mr. Patient has AD. However, he needs a neurological work-up for dementia before the clinical diagnosis can be established conclusively.

Capacity Findings:

1. **Probable current incapacity to enter into contracts.** This incapacity would include loan agreements, real estate contracts, and corporate buy/sell agreements.

The history, interview information, and test data indicated that Mr. Patient is probably incapable currently of entering into contracts such as the proposed buy-sell agreement. Ms. Daughter reported that her father has recently sold some real estate at a fraction of what it is worth. She said that he has also made several large loans to his business recently but seems generally unaware of these loans and the fact that they are not being repaid. He had very little specific knowledge regarding the proposed buy-sell agreement and seemed confused about its purpose.

Contractual capacity is a higher order legal test which draws upon a variety of cognitive abilities, including memory, conceptual knowledge, reading ability, mental flexibility/executive function, and judgment. As discussed above, Mr. Patient is suffering from a moderate progressive dementia, probably of the Alzheimer's type, and he currently demonstrates significant deficits in all cognitive domains tested, including attention, memory, comprehension, and executive function. Screening for reading abilities revealed that Mr. Patient currently reads at the 2nd grade level (2%ile for age), which reflects a decline from estimated premorbid levels.

In the examiner's opinion, Mr. Patient no longer possesses the abilities to read and comprehend contractual documents, to recall essential information and details about contractual matters, to have the mental flexibility and judgment to negotiate effectively, or to make such business decisions in his best interest. In summary, he is no longer capable of entering into contracts, and it is likely that he has lacked this capacity for several years.

2. Probable current incapacity to make a new will.

Interview and test data indicated that Mr. Patient is probably incapable currently of making a new will. Mr. Patient was unable to provide an adequate description of a will, stating only "It's where you put stuff in different people's names." He was also unable to set forth the nature and extent of his property to be listed within a will, describing his assets initially only as "farmland." When specifically prompted about items of property including his business, home, bank accounts, and stocks, he stated that he wanted these things to go to his children. When asked about debts owed to him, he stated that no one owed him any money. When reminded that he had loaned money to his business, and that repayment of these loans could be made to his estate after his death, he acknowledged that these debts were still outstanding. However, he could not recall the exact amount of the loans. Mr. Patient's lack of knowledge of assets/property to be passed in his will was also reflected in his poor performance on Domain 8 of the FCI-9, which tests general knowledge of personal assets and estate arrangements.

Mr. Patient did know the objects of his bounty and did indicate a general plan of distribution, stating that he would want his property to pass to his children equally. However, on testing, Mr. Patient indicated that he had not yet made a will, whereas his daughter reported that he has a current will.
It is the examiner's judgment that Mr. Patient currently lacks testamentary capacity.

3. Probable current incapacity to manage business-related and everyday financial affairs.

History, interview, and test data indicated that Mr. Patient is also currently incapable of managing his overall financial affairs and making business-related decisions. In interview, Mr. Patient demonstrated inaccurate knowledge of his financial and business affairs. For example, the patient indicated that he goes into work at his excavation business every day, even occasionally running construction equipment, whereas the patient's daughter reported that he is retired and that his brother operates and manages the business on his own. She reported that her father continues to manage his own finances, though she sometimes helps with bill-paying, and he makes poor business decisions (e.g., recently sold some property for 10% of what it was worth). She reported that her father has agreed several times not to sign anything without letting her review it first, but then forgets to consult her.

Functional testing of financial abilities revealed overall severe impairment in financial capacity. On testing, Mr. Patient demonstrated intact performance on tasks of naming coins/currency, coin/currency relationships, and single and multi-item cash purchases. However, he was impaired on tests of counting coins/currency, understanding financial concepts, making change for a vending machine, tipping, conceptual understanding of a checkbook, use of a checkbook, conceptual understanding of a bank statement, use of a bank statement, detection of telephone fraud, conceptual understanding of bills, identifying and prioritizing bills, knowledge of personal financial activities, and investment decision making. Taken together, these findings indicate that he is no longer capable of managing any aspect of his business and financial affairs.

4. **Probable vulnerability to undue influence.**

In addition to his capacity impairment, it is very likely that Mr. Patient is currently vulnerable to undue influence in his business and other activities. Early on in their disease course, as their short-term memory and comprehension abilities erode, patients with AD become increasingly vulnerable to the influence of others. It is likely that Mr. Patient's reported recent poor business decisions may reflect such a vulnerability. For example, during testing Mr. Patient failed to detect a telephone credit card scam situation and agreed to provide his credit card number over the phone to an unknown caller.

RECOMMENDATIONS

1. We recommend that Mr. Patient be referred to the UAB Memory Disorders Clinic for a full neurological and dementia evaluation.
2. Continued pharmacotherapy with cholinesterase inhibitors appears to be appropriate.
3. Mr. Patient and his family should consider legally securing his business, financial, and personal affairs as soon as possible, either by his daughter acting as his agent under Mr. Patient's power of attorney, or if that does not work, by seeking a guardianship and conservatorship.
4. Mr. Patient's cognitive and emotional status should continue to be closely monitored. This evaluation would provide a useful baseline if follow-up testing were indicated.

The results of this evaluation are confidential.

C. Note on Post-Assessment Action by the Attorney

Based on this assessment, Mr. Patient's attorney concluded that he should not proceed in doing Mr. Patient's will, nor with execution of the buy-sell agreement. The attorney informed Mr. Patient of the assessment results and provided a copy to Mr. Patient and, with his permission, to his daughter. (If Mr. Patient had not given permission, the attorney would have to determine whether disclosure might be a necessary action to protect the legal interests of his client under Model Rule 1.14.)

The attorney advised Mr. Patient and his daughter that it is time for his daughter to handle his financial affairs as his legal agent. The attorney provided the daughter with a background brochure explaining the responsibilities and tips for carrying out the responsibilities of a fiduciary under a durable power of attorney. Finally, the attorney reinforced the assessor's recommendation for referral to the UAB Memory Disorders Clinic.

Attachment to Assessment Report—Test Scores

DOMAIN	TEST	Raw	Scaled/Index	%ile
Dementia Severity	DRS-2 Total	89	2ss	<1
Attention	DRS-2 Attention	29	4ss	2
Receptive Language	WAB-R Auditory Verbal Comp.	57		<1
Memory	DRS-2 Memory	9	2ss	<1
	CVLT-3 Trials Sum of Scaled Scores	21	64SS	1
	CVLT-3 List B	1	5ss	5
	CVLT-3 Total Delayed Recall Index	0	50ss	<1
	CVLT-3 Total Recall Index	32	53SS	<1
	CVLT-3 Recognition Discriminability	0.3	3ss	1
	CVLT-3 Total Repetitions	0	15ss	95
	CVLT-3 Total Intrusions	5	10ss	50
Visuospatial	DRS-2 Construction	6	10ss	41-59
	CLOX 2	11		
Abstraction/Judgment	DRS-2 Conceptualization	24	3ss	1
	TOP-J	7		
Executive Function	DRS-2 Initialization/Perseveration	21	2ss	<1
	Trails A seconds (errors)	161 (5)		2
	Trails B seconds (errors)	>300 (8)		<1
	CLOX 1	8		
	Token Test	8		
Mood/Personality	Geriatric Depression Scale	0		
Achievement	WRAT-5 Word Reading	27	(Grade:2)	2
Additional Tests	FCI-9 Domain 1 Total	43	-0.73	23
	FCI-9 Domain 2 Total	10/23		
	FCI-9 Domain 3 Total	17	-2.53	<1
	FCI-9 Domain 4 Total	19	-30.20	<1
	FCI-9 Domain 5 Total	2	-5.84	<1
	FCI-9 Domain 6 Task 6C	0	-9.54	<1
	FCI-9 Domain 7 Total	11/19		
	FCI-9 Domain 8 Total	12	-3.04	<1
	FCI-9 Domain 9 Total	5	-3.75	<1

Appendix 3. Medical Conditions Affecting Capacity[1]

Dementia is a general term for a medical condition characterized by a loss of memory and functioning. Primary degenerative dementias are those with disease processes that result in a deteriorating course, including Alzheimer's disease, Lewy Body Dementia, and Frontal Dementia (each associated with a type of abnormal brain cell).

Condition	Etiology	Symptoms	Treatability
Alcoholic Dementia	A fairly common form of dementia, caused by long-term abuse of alcohol, usually for 20 years or more. Alcohol is a neurotoxin that passes the blood-brain barrier.	Memory loss, problem- solving difficulty, and impairments in visuospatial function are commonly found in patients with alcohol dementia.	Alcohol dementia is partially reversible, if there is long-term sobriety—cessation of use. There is evidence to suggest that some damaged brain tissue may regenerate following extended sobriety, leading to modest improvements in thinking and function.
Alzheimer's disease ("AD")	Most common type of dementia, caused by a progressive brain disease involving protein deposits in brain and disruption of neurotransmitter systems.	Initial short-term memory loss, followed by problems in language and communication, orientation to time and place, everyday problem solving, and eventually recognition of people and everyday objects. In the early stages, an individual may retain some decisional and functional abilities.	Progressive and irreversible, resulting ultimately in a terminal state. Medications may improve symptoms and cause a temporary brightening of function in the earlier stages.
Bipolar Disorder or Manic Depression	A psychiatric illness characterized by alternating periods of mania and depression.	May affect functional and decisional abilities in the manic stage or when the depressed stage is severe.	Can be treated with medication but requires a strong commitment to treatment on the part of the individual. Varies over time; periodic re-evaluation is needed.

[1] This Appendix is used with permission from *Assessment of Older Adults with Diminished Capacity: Handbook for Psychologists*, copyright by the ABA Commission on Law and Aging and the American Psychological Association (2005). The list is meant to define terms **as used in this** book and is not meant to define terms more universally. The glossary uses definitions from the *Diagnostic and Statistical Manual of Mental Disorders*, where available, and where not, definitions are based on the consensus of the working group.

Condition	Etiology	Symptoms	Treatability
Coma	A state of temporary or permanent unconsciousness.	Minimally responsive or unresponsive, unable to communicate decisions and needs a substitute decision maker.	Often temporary; regular re-evaluation required.
Delirium	A temporary confusional state with a wide variety of causes, such as dehydration, poor nutrition, multiple medication use, medication reaction, anesthesia, metabolic imbalances, and infections.	Substantially impaired attention and significant decisional and functional impairments across many domains. May be difficult to distinguish from the confusion and inattention characteristic of dementia.	Often temporary and reversible. If untreated may proceed to a dementia. It is important to rule out delirium before diagnosing dementia. To do so, a good understanding of the history and course of functional decline, as well as a full medical work-up, are necessary.
Frontal or Frontotemporal Dementia (Pick's disease is one example)	Broad category of dementia caused by brain diseases or small strokes that affect the frontal lobes of the brain.	Problems with personality and behavior are often the first changes, followed by problems in organization, judgment, insight, motivation, and the ability to engage in goal-oriented behavior.	Early in their disease, patients may have areas of retained functional ability, but as disease progresses, they can rapidly lose all decisional capacity.
Jacob-Creutzfeldt Disease	A rare type of progressive dementia affecting humans that is related to "mad cow" disease.	The disease usually has a rapid course, with death occurring within two years of initial symptoms. These include fatigue, mental slowing, depression, bizarre ideations, confusion, and motor disturbances, including muscular jerking, leading finally to a vegetative state and death.	There is no treatment currently and the disease is relentlessly progressive.
Diffuse Lewy Body Dementia (DLB)	A type of dementia on the Parkinson disease spectrum.	DLB involves mental changes that precede or co-occur with motor changes. Visual hallucinations are	This disease is progressive and there are no known treatments. Parkinson medications are often of limited use.

Condition	Etiology	Symptoms	Treatability
		common, as are fluctuations in mental capacity.	
Major Depression	A very common psychiatric illness.	Sad or disinterested mood, poor appetite, energy, sleep, and concentration, feelings of hopelessness, helplessness, and suicidality. In severe cases, poor hygiene, hallucinations, delusions, and impaired decisional and functional abilities.	Treatable and reversible, although in some resistant cases electroconvulsive therapy (ECT) is needed.
Developmental Disorders ("DD"), including Mental Retardation ("MR")	Brain-related conditions that begin at birth or childhood (before age 18) and continue throughout adult life. MR concerns low-level intellectual functioning with functional deficits that can be found across many kinds of DD, including autism, Down syndrome, and cerebral palsy.	Functioning tends to be stable over time but lower than normal peers. MR is most commonly mild. Some conditions such as Downs syndrome may develop a supervening dementia later in life, causing decline in already limited decisional and functional abilities.	Not reversible, but everyday functioning can be improved with a wide range of supports, interventions, and less restrictive alternatives. Individuals with DD have a wide range of decisional and functional abilities and, thus, require careful assessment by skilled clinicians.
Parkinson's Disease (PD)	Progressive brain disease that initially affects motor function, but in many cases proceeds to dementia.	PD presents initially with problems with tremors and physical movement, followed by problems with expression and thinking, and leading sometimes to dementia after a number of years.	PD is progressive, but motor symptoms can be treated for many years. Eventually, medications become ineffective and most physical and mental capacities are lost. Evaluation of capacity must avoid confusion of physical for cognitive impairment.
Persistent Vegetative State (PSV)	A state of minimal or no responsiveness following emergence from coma.	Patient is mute and immobile with an absence of all higher mental activity. Cannot communicate decisions and requires a substitute decision maker for all areas.	Cases of PSV usually lead to death within a year's time.

Condition	Etiology	Symptoms	Treatability
Schizophrenia	A chronic brain-based psychiatric illness	Hallucinations and delusions; poor judgment, insight, planning, personal hygiene, interpersonal skills. May range from mild to severe. Impact on functional and decisional abilities is variable.	Many symptoms can be successfully treated with medication. Capacity loss may occur when patients go off their medications.
Stroke or Cerebral Vascular Accident ("CVA")	A significant bleeding in the brain, or a blockage of oxygen to the brain.	May affect just one part of the brain, so individuals should be carefully assessed to determine their functional and decisional abilities.	Some level of recovery and improved function over the first year; thus, a temporary guardianship might be considered if the stroke is recent.
Traumatic Brain Injury ("TBI")	A blow to the head that usually involves loss of consciousness.	Individuals with mild and moderate TBI may appear superficially the same as before the accident, but have persisting problems with motivation, judgment, and organization. Those with severe TBI may have profound problems with everyday functioning.	Usually show recovery of thinking and functional abilities over the first year; thus, a temporary guardianship should be considered if the injury is recent.
Vascular Cognitive Impairment	Multiple infarcts that cause cognitive impairment	Functional strengths and weaknesses may vary, depending on the extent and location of the strokes.	May remain stable over time if underlying cerebrovascular or heart disease is successfully managed.
Vascular Dementia ("VaD")	Multiple strokes that accumulate and cause dementia.	Functional strengths and weaknesses may vary, depending on the extent and location of the strokes.	May worsen if cerebrovascular disease continues to cause progressive impairment.

Appendix 4: The Brain in Aging and Disease

Legal professionals should be familiar with how human brains change as they age. Research has described "age related changes in cognition." These are described below. They were discovered in studies of persons who did not have diseases or other conditions that are known to affect cognition and mental health. Importantly, there are other causes of cognitive and behavioral impairment (e.g., developmental or intellectual disabilities) not described below that legal professionals should also be familiar with when working with older adults. This section will focus on the more common changes to cognition in later life.

Briefly summarized, selected cognitive abilities decline as we grow older, particularly after the 5th decade. These are categorized as "fluid abilities." The term described a set of cognitive abilities that use attention, memory, and problem solving. These abilities affect how well we can pay attention in a conversation, multitask, and use new information to solve a problem. Usually, we adapt to these changes. For example, someone who experiences age-related declines in fluid intelligence may have trouble remembering all the items she intended to pick up from the grocery store and so she will use a list and may take longer to do the shopping. There is substantial variability in the rate and magnitude of these changes. A category of cognitive abilities that does not decline with age are the "crystallized abilities." This term described the knowledge of facts, such as words and their meaning, procedures, and skills. Over time, crystallized intelligence remains static or increases, as for example, people can expand their vocabulary.

In addition to aging, medical and psychiatric conditions can affect an older client's cognitive functioning. If they do, their impact in capacity is often greater than that seen with aging. Notably as well, age-related changes in brain cells make older adults more vulnerable to the harms of medical and psychiatric conditions. For example, an acute infection can cause delirium and anxiety can cause inattention. Legal professionals should be aware of signs of confusion that would warrant caution and perhaps further investigation from a health professional. Common signs include repetitious questions, forgetting recent information and, as reported by the person, feeling suddenly "less sharp" or "foggy." Importantly, these clinical evaluations can determine if the cognitive difficulty experienced by a client is due to the aging process, and thus normal for that person, or due to some other abnormal process.

One common cause of cognitive decline in older adults is dementia. Dementia describes problems with multiple cognitive abilities that impair a person's day to day function. It is not normal aging. A person with dementia is, at least to some degree, disabled. Cognitive impairments may be observed in memory, executive function, attention, language, spatial abilities, or other areas. There are many causes of dementia. One of the most common are brain diseases, such as Alzheimer's disease and Lewy body diseases. These causes of dementia produce different patterns of cognitive impairment and progress at different rates. They are similar in that they impact how well a person functions in his or her day-to-day life, such as driving, shopping, managing money, and cooking. Dementias are progressive, meaning they will get worse over time, though the rate of progression is quite variable from person to person. Individuals living with dementia need support from others (commonly called "caregivers"), and, as the disease advances, this support becomes more and more all-encompassing. In later stages, a person needs help with eating, dressing, and bathing.

Importantly, in recent years the term **Major Neurocognitive Disorder** has emerged and is now found in the fifth edition of the Diagnostic and Statistical Manual of Mental Disorders (DSM-5) as the new term for dementia (although we are likely still to hear both terms used). This term reflects the wealth of new information about the biological underpinnings of dementia. It also sets aside the stigma attached to "dementia." Legal professionals may also encounter the term **Mild Neurocognitive Disorder** or **Mild Cognitive Impairment**. These terms describe declines in cognitive functioning that are greater than expected for one's age but not to such an extent that the person is unable to perform important tasks to living independently. They are less efficient. For example, an older client may have more trouble with memory than would be expected, but has demonstrated an ability to still drive safely, shop, and prepare their own meals.

Advances in biology have not replaced an essential fact: To diagnose dementia or major neurocognitive disorder, or mild cognitive impairment, or mild neurocognitive disorder, a clinical evaluation is needed. Because of the ever-evolving research and practice in diagnosis and labels, legal professionals wanting to learn more are encouraged to review the suggested resources.

Suggested Resources

National Institute on Aging - www.nia.nih.gov
Information and handouts on various topics of aging, including dementia

Alzheimer's Association - www.alz.org
Information and handouts about different causes of dementia
Annual publication on facts and figures, as well as special topics related to dementia

Institute of Medicine - https://doi.org/10.17226/21693
Cognitive aging: Progress in understanding and opportunities for action. (2015).

Center for Disease Control and Prevention - www.cdc.gov/aging/dementia
Information on Alzheimer's Disease and related dementias.

Endnotes

[1] *2019 Alzheimer's Disease Facts and Figures*, Alzheimer's Ass'n 17 (2019), https://www.alz.org/media/documents/alzheimers-facts-and-figures-2019-r.pdf.

[2] *Id,* at P. 9, Table 2.

[3] *Id. See also* Francis T. Hane et al., *Recent Progress in Alzheimer's Disease Research, Part 3: Diagnosis and Treatment*, 57,3 J. Alzheimer's Disease 645 (2017).

[4] Am. Bar Ass'n Commission on L. & Aging, *Supporting Decision Making Across the Age Spectrum* (March 2020), https://www.americanbar.org/content/dam/aba/administrative/law_aging/2020-supporting-decision-making-final-report.pdf.

[5] , *e.g.,* Robert D. Dinerstein, *Implementing Legal Capacity Under Article 12 of the UN Convention on the Rights of Persons with Disabilities: The Difficult Road from Guardianship to Supported Decision-Making*, 19 Hum. Rts. Brief, Winter 2012, at 8, 10; *see also* Jonathan G. Martinis, *Supported Decision-Making: Protecting Rights, Ensuring Choices*, BiFocal 36:5, p. 109 (2015), https://www.americanbar.org/groups/law_aging/publications/bifocal/vol_36/issue_5_june2015/supported-decision-making.

[6] Am. Bar Ass'n Commission on L. & Aging, *supra* note 4, at 2.

[7] Model Rules of Prof'l Conduct r. 1.14 cmt. 6 (Am. Bar Ass'n 2019).

[8] The factors contained in this Comment to Rule 1.14 derive from Peter Margulies, *Access, Connection, and Voice: A Contextual Approach to Representing Senior Citizens of Questionable Capacity*, 62 Fordham L. Rev. 1073 (1994), part of a symposium issue of articles and recommendations of the National Conference on Ethical Issues in Representing Older Clients.

[9] Martin D. Begleiter, *The Gambler Breaks Even: Legal Malpractice in Complicated Estate Planning Cases*, 20 Ga. St. U. L. Rev. 277, 314 (2003).

[10] Privity requirement, 3 *Modern Tort Law: Liability and Litigation* § 25:24 (2d ed.).

[11] *See* Arthur C. Walsh, Baird B. Brown, Kathryn Kaye, & James Grigsby, *Mental Capacity: Legal and Medical Aspects of Assessment and Treatment* (2d ed. 1999 & Supp. 2019) for a discussion of the case law concerning the lawyer's malpractice liability for knowingly allowing an incapacitated person to execute legal documents.

[12] State terminology varies. In this Handbook, the generic term "guardianship" refers to guardians of the person as well as guardians of the property, frequently called "conservators" unless otherwise indicated.

[13] Robert D. Dinerstein, *supra* note 5, at 8.

[14] As of the beginning of 2021, ten jurisdictions had enacted Supported Decision-Making Agreements laws (Alaska, Delaware, District of Columbia, Indiana, Louisiana, Nevada, North Dakota, Rhode Island, Texas, and Wisconsin). *See also* Zachary Allen & Dari Pogach, *More States Pass Supported Decision-Making Agreement Laws*, 41 Bifocal J. ABA Commission on L. & Aging, 136, 159 (2019). https://www.americanbar.org/groups/law_aging/publications/bifocal/vol-41/volume-41-issue-1/where-states-stand-on-supported-decision-making/

[15] Am. Bar Ass'n Commission on L. & Aging, supra note 4, at 2.

[16] *See* Haldan Blecher, *Least Restrictive Alternatives in State Guardianship Statutes*, Am. Bar Ass'n Commission on L. & Aging, www.americanbar.org/content/dam/aba/administrative/law_aging/06-23-2018-lra-chart-final.pdf (last updated June 23, 2018).

[17] *See* Adult Guardianship Legislation Summary(annual), American Bar Association Commission on Law and Aging, https://www.americanbar.org/groups/law_aging/resources/guardianship_law_practice/ (scroll to "State Laws & Policy").

[18] Unif. Guardianship, Conservatorship, & Other Protective Arrangements Act § 301(a)(1)(A) (Unif. Law Comm'n 2017).

[19] *See,* Jenica Cassidy, *Restoration of Rights in the Termination of Adult Guardianship,* 23 Elder L.J. 83 (2015).

[20] *See* Convention on the Rights of Persons with Disabilities, Article 12, *opened for signature* Mar. 30, 2007, 2515 U.N.T.S. 3 [hereinafter CRPD].

[21] See *generally,* Kristin Booth Glen, *Supported Decision-Making and the Human Right of Legal Capacity*, 3 Inclusion 2; and Kristin Booth Glen, *Introducing a "New" Human Right: Learning from Others, Bringing Legal Capacity Home*, 49 Colum. Hum. Rts. Rev. 1 (2018).

[22] Charles P. Sabatino and Erica Wood, *The Conceptualization of Legal Capacity of Older Persons in Western Law*, in Beyond Elder Law: New Directions in Law and Aging, 35, 37-39 (Israel Doron & Ann M. Soden eds, 2012). *See also* Am. Bar Ass'n Comm'n on Law & Aging & Sally Balch Hurme, *Capacity Definition & Initiation of Guardianship Proceedings*, Am. Bar Ass'n Commission on L. & Aging, www.americanbar.org/content/dam/aba/administrative/law_aging/chartcapacityandinitiation.pdf (Last updated August 2020).;

[23] *See, e.g.,* Va. Code Ann. §64.2-2000 (2020).

[24] Unif. Guardianship, Conservatorship, & Other Protective Arrangements Act § 301(a) (Unif. Law Comm'n 2017).

[25] *See, e.g., id.* §102(16) (defining "limited guardianship" as "a guardianship that grants the guardian less than all powers available under this [act] or otherwise restricts the powers of the guardian").

[26] *See, e.g., id.* §310(c) (providing strong language for limited guardianship: a court establishing a full guardianship for an adult must state the basis for granting a full guardianship and include specific findings that support the conclusion that a limited guardianship would not meet the functional needs of the adult...." A court establishing a limited guardianship must state the specific powers granted to the guardian).

[27] Debra Chopp, *Addressing Cultural Bias in the Legal Profession*, 41 N.Y.U. Rev. L. & Soc. Change 367, 378 (2015).

[28] Sue Bryant & Jean Joh Peters, *Five Habits of Cross Lawyering*, Yale Univ. (1999). http://fivehabitsandmore.law.yale.edu/jean-and-sues-materials/habits.

[29] *Project Implicit*, Harvard University, https://implicit.harvard.edu/implicit/selectatest.html. For more information about Project Implicit, see https://implicit.harvard.edu/implicit/aboutus.html.

[30] *See* Nation Swell Studio & AARP, *Confronting Unconscious Age Bias*, Nation Swell (July 31, 2019), https://nationswell.com/campaigns/confronting-unconscious-age-bias/, for tips on confronting and addressing age bias, https://nationswell.com/campaigns/confronting-unconscious-age-bias/.

[31] *See* Am. Bar Ass'n Comm'n on Law & Aging et al., *PRACTICAL Tool*, A.B.A. Commission on L. & Aging, (May 9, 2016), https://ambar.org/practicaltool.

[32] Americans with Disabilities Act (ADA) § 36.104, 28 C.F.R. § 36.104 (2018); *see also*, David Godfrey, Adrienne Lyon Buenavista, & Danielle Valdenaire, *Checklist for an Elder-Friendly Law Office* (ABA Commission on Law and Aging 2013), https://www.americanbar.org/groups/law_aging/resources/ethics_and_counseling_older_clients.

[33] Linda F. Smith, *Representing the Elderly Client and Addressing the Question of Competence*, 14 J. of Contemporary L. 61 at 90 & 92 (1988).

[34] 17 C.J.S. *Contracts* § 45 (2020).

[35] 17A C.J.S. *Contracts* § 191 (2020).

[36] 26A C.J.S. *Deeds* § 98 (2020).

[37] Restatement (Third) of Property (Wills & Don. Trans.) § 8.1(c) (Am. 2003).

[38] *See, e.g.,* John Parry & F. Phillips Gilliam, *Handbook on Mental Disability Law* 147-48 (2002).

[39] Carmelle Peisah & Henry Brodaty, *Dementia and the Will-making Process: The Role of the Medical Practitioner*, 161 Medical J. of Australia 381 (September 19, 1994).

[40] Restatement (Third) of Property, *supra* note 37.

[41] Unif. Guardianship, Conservatorship & Other Protective Arrangements Act §401 (Unif. Law Comm'n 2017).

[42] Eric Widera, Veronika Steenpass, Daniel Marson, & Rebecca Sudore, *Finances in the Older Patient with Cognitive Impairment: "He didn't want me to take over"*, 305(7) JAMA 698, 699 (2011).

[43] *See* Daniel C. Marson et al., *Clinical Interview Assessment of Financial Capacity in Older Adults with Mild Cognitive Impairment and Alzheimer's Disease*, 57(5) J. Am. Geriatric Soc'y 806, 807 (2009) (discussing the semi-structured clinical interview for evaluating seven core financial domains and overall financial capacity (Semi-Structured Clinical Interview for Financial Capacity; SCIFC)). Other capacity tests that include financial measures include the Independent Living Scales (ILS), the Direct Assessment of Functional Skills (DAFS), and the Structured Assessment of Independent Living Skills (SAILS).

[44] Unif. Health-Care Decisions Act, §1(3) (Unif. Law Comm'n 1993).

[45] Thomas Grisso & Paul S. Appelbaum, *Assessing Competence to Consent to Treatment: A Guide for Physicians and Other Health Professionals* (1998); Loren H. Roth, Alan Meisel, & Charles W. Lidz, *Tests of Competency to Consent to Treatment*, 134(3) Amer. J. Psychiatry 279 (1977).

[46] *See e.g.*, Michele J. Karel, Ronald J. Gurrera, Bret Hicken, & Jennifer Moye, *Reasoning in the Capacity to Make Medical Decisions: The Consideration of Values*, 21(1) J. Clin. Ethics 58 (Spring 2010).

[47] *See* Lawrence A. Frolik & Mary F. Radford, *"Sufficient" Capacity: The Contrasting Capacity Requirements for Different Documents*, 2 N.A.E.L.A.J. 303, 313 (2006).

[48] *E.g.,* Cal. Prob. Code § 4120 (West 1994).

[49] Jennifer Moye, Charles P. Sabatino & Rebecca Weintraub Brendel, *Evaluation of the Capacity to Appoint a Healthcare Proxy*, 21(4) Am. J Geriatric Psychiatry 326, 332-333 (2013).

[50] Maynard v. Hill, 125 U.S. 190, 212 (1888).

[51] *See, e.g.,* Vivian E. Hamilton, *The Age of Marital Capacity: Reconsidering Civil Recognition of Adolescent Marriage*, 92 B.U. L. Rev. 1817, 1828 (2012); Members of the Common-Law Tests of Capacity Project Comm., *Report on Common Law Tests of Capacity,* 73 B.C. L. Inst. 1, 178 (2013).

[52] *Id.* at 1828.

[53] *See, e.g.*, Durahm v. Durahm, 10 PD 80, 82 (Eng Probate Division 1855); Members of the Common-Law Tests of Capacity Project Comm., *supra* note 51, at 18-19 (historically the common law standard has been low. The test always had the goal of supporting autonomy and protecting the vulnerable but keeping in mind the risk of predatory marriages. Legal experts caution that the test should not be set too high or it denies people with diminished capacity the right to marry, which might otherwise enrich their lives).

[54] Robert G. Robinson, *Mental Disability and the Law in Canada* 253-254 (2d 1994). *See also,* Emily Clough & Michael Larsen, *The (not so) simple Contract: Mental Capacity & the Act of Marriage,* at 6 (November 3, 2017) (unpublished manuscript) (on file with Clark Wilson LLP); Banton v. Banton, 164 D.L.R. 4th 176, at para. 157 (Ont. Gen. Div, 1998) (finding that the ability to consider property rights and obligations was not an essential component of the test for marital capacity).

[55] M.C. Dransfield, Annotation, *Capacity to Marry*, 82 A.L.R.2d 1040 (citing Johnson v. Johnson, 104 N.W.2d 8 (N.D. 1960)).

[56] Unif. Marriage & Divorce Act § 208(a)(1) (Unif. Law Comm'n 1996) cmt. ("Courts construing the 'lacks capacity to consent' language of Subsection (a)(1) will undoubtedly continue to apply existing stringent standards by holding that a declaration of invalidity is appropriate only if the petitioner offers

clear and definite evidence that one of the spouses lacked "sufficient mental capacity to understand intelligently the marriage contract…and the obligations it imposed on him")

[57] *See* Robinson *supra* note 54, at 254. *See also* Devore-Thompson v. Poulain, 2017 BCSC 1289; Johnson v. Sands, 124 S.W.2d 774 (Ky. Ct. App. 1939); Baughman v. Baughman, 4 P. 1003 (Kan. 1884).

[58] *See* Nick O'Neil and Carmelle Peisah, Capacity and the Law at 9 (2011).

[59] *See* Johnson v. Sands, 124 S.W.2d 774 (Ky. Ct. App. 1939).

[60] *Id.* at 775.

[61] Benjamin N. Cardozo Sch. of Law & Cardozo Journal of Conflict Resolution, *ADA Mediation Guidelines* 7 (2000). https://cardozojcr.com/ada-mediation-guidelines.

[62] *See, e.g.,* Patrick G. Coy & Tim Hedeen, *Disabilities and Mediation Readiness in Court-Referred Cases: Developing Screening Criteria and Service Networks*, 16 Mediation Q. 113, 120 (1998).

[63] *See* Erica F. Wood, *Dispute Resolution & Dementia: Seeking Solutions*, 35 Ga. L. Rev. 785, 814 (2001).

[64] Fed. R. Evid. 603, cmt.

[65] *Id.*

[66] *See, e.g.,* Kevin M. Cremin et al., *Ensuring a Fair Hearing for Litigants with Mental Illness: The Law and Psychology of Capacity, Admissibility, and Credibility Assessments in Civil Proceedings*, 17 J. L. & Pol'y 455, 461 (2009).

[67] Fed. R. Evid. 603.

[68] *See, e.g.,* Kevin M. Cremin et al., *supra* note 66, at 462 (citing District of Columbia. v. Armes, 107 U.S. 519, 521-22 (1883)); People v. Rensing, 14 N.Y.2d 210, 213 (N.Y. 1964); Ellarson v. Ellarson, 190 N.Y.S. 6, 8 (N.Y. App. Div. 1921).

[69] *See* Stephanie L. Tang, *When "Yes" Might Mean "No": Standardizing State Criteria to Evaluate the Capacity to Consent to Sexual Activity for Elderly with Neurocognitive Disorders*, 22 Elder Law J. 449, 468 (2015).

[70] *Id.*, at 471-474.

[71] American Bar Association Commission on Law and Aging & American Psychological Association, *Assessment of Older Adults with Diminished Capacity: A Handbook for Psychologists* 62-63 (2008), http://www.apa.org/pi/aging/programs/assessment/capacity-psychologist-handbook.pdf.

[72] *See* Alfredo Nicolosi et al., *Sexual Behavior and Sexual Dysfunctions After Age 40: The Global Study of Sexual Attitudes and Behaviors*, 64 Urology 991-997. (2004).

[73] *See* Michael Bauer et al., *'I Always Look Under the Bed tor a Man'. Needs and Barriers to the Expression of Sexuality in Residential Aged Care: The Views of Residents with and without Dementia*, 4 Psychology & Sexuality 296 (2013); Susan M. Benbow & Derek Beeston, *Sexuality, Aging, and Dementia,* 24 International Psychogeriatrics 1026 (2012).

[74] *See* Terrie B. Ginsberg, Sherry C. Pomerantz, & Veronika Kramer-Felley, *Sexuality in older adults: Behaviors and Preferences*. 34 Age and Ageing 475 (2005).

[75] *See* Carmelle Peisah, Jay Luxenberg, Benjamin Liptzin, Anne P. Wand, Kenneth Shulman & Sanford Finkel, *Deathbed Wills: Assessing Testamentary Capacity in the Dying Patient*, 26(2) Int'l Psychogeriatric 209 (2014).

[76] Johnson v. Olson (*In re* Estate of Olson), 19 Cal. App. 379, 386 (Cal. Dist. Ct. App. 1912).

[77] *See, e.g.,* Lisa Nerenberg, *An Interview with Margaret Singer on Undue Influence* (March 1996), https://www.elderjusticecal.org/uploads/1/0/1/7/101741090/nexus_interview_with_margaret_singer.pdf; Mary Joy Quinn, *Friendly Persuasion, Good Salesmanship, or Undue Influence*, 2 Marquette Elder's Advisor 49 (2001); Lisa Nerenberg, *Literature Review on Undue Influence*, in Mary Joy Quinn, Eileen

Goldman & Lisa Nerenberg, *Undue Influence: Definitions and Applications*, Appendix C (March 2010), https://www.courts.ca.gov/documents/UndueInfluence.pdf.

[78] *See, e.g.*, Bonnie Brandl, Candace J. Heisler & Lori A. Stiegel, *The Parallels Between Undue Influence, Domestic Violence, Stalking, and Sexual Assault*, 17 J. Elder Abuse & Neglect 37 (2005); Steven Hassan, & Mansi Jitendra Shah, *The Anatomy of Undue Influence Used by Terrorist Cults and Traffickers to Induce Helplessness and Trauma, so Creating False Identities*, 8 Ethics, Med. & Pub. Health 97 (2019); *Undue Influence: Definitions and Applications*, *supra* note 77, at 10.

[79] *See* Lori A. Stiegel & Mary Joy Quinn, Elder Abuse: The Impact of Undue Influence: Issue Brief 2 (National Center on Law and Elder Rights 2017), https://ncler.acl.gov/pdf/Advanced-Elder-Abuse-The-Impact-of-Undue-Influence.pdf.

[80] *See* Michael B. McNaughton & Agatha Christies, *Proving a Will Contest Through Circumstantial Evidence,* 8(2) California Trusts and Estates Quarterly 35 (2010).

[81] Interview with Mary Joy Quinn, Director of the San Francisco Probate Court (Feb. 25, 2020).

[82] Am. Bar Ass'n Comm'n on Law & Aging & Am. Psychological Ass'n, *supra* note 71, at 114.

[83] Restatement (Second) of Contracts §177 (Am. Law Inst. 1981).

[84] Am. Bar Ass'n Comm'n on Law & Aging & Am. Psychological Ass'n, *supra* note 71, at 113.

[85] Margaret T. Singer, *Cults in Our Midst* (1995).

[86] Bennett Blum, Undue Influence-Behavior Models, http://www.bennettblummd.com/.

[87] Susan Bernatz, The Bernatz SCAM Model. http://www.bernatzexperts.com.

[88] Brandl, Bonnie, Heisler, Candace, Stiegel, Lori, Undue Influence: *The Parallels Between Undue Influence, Domestic Violence, Stalking, & Sexual Assault,* 17 J. Elder Abuse & Neglect 37, 43-48 (2005).

[89] B.C. L. Inst., Recommended Practices for Wills Practitioners Relating to Potential Undue Influence: A Guide (2011). http://www.lawsociety.bc.ca/docs/practice/resources/guide-wills.pdf.

[90] Cal. Prob. Code §86 (West 2020); Cal. Welf. & Inst. Code §15610.70 (West 2020).

[91] Mary Joy Quinn, Lisa Nerenberg, Adria Navarro. & Kathleen Wilber, *Developing An Undue Influence Screening Tool for Adult Protective Services*. 29 J. Elder Abuse & Neglect 157 (2017).

[92] *Id. See also* Mary Joy Quinn, Lisa Nerenberg, Adria Navarro. & Kathleen Wilber, *Developing an Undue Influence Screening Tool for Adult Protective Services: Final Report to the Borchard Foundation Center on Law and Aging* (May 27, 2016). https://www.elderjusticecal.org/uploads/1/0/1/7/101741090/developing_an_undue_influence_screening_tool_for_adult_protective_services_7.5.16.pdf.

[93] Cal. Prob. Code §86 (West 2020); Cal. Welf. & Inst. Code §15610.70 (West 2020).

[94] Am. Bar Ass'n Comm'n on Law & Aging et al., *PRACTICAL Tool*, *supra* note 31.

[95] *See* Nat'l Acad. of Elder Law Attorneys, *Aspirational Standards for the Practice of Elder Law and Special Needs Law*, Standard B.3.(2d ed. 2017). *See also*, Am. Bar Ass'n Comm'n on Law & Aging, *Why Am I Left in the Waiting Room: Understanding the Four Cs of Elder Law Ethics*, A.B.A. Commission on Law & Aging (2020), https://www.americanbar.org/content/dam/aba/administrative/law_aging/2020-elderlaw-ethics-brochure.pdf.

[96] See Margulies, *supra* note 8.

[97] *See, e.g.,* Scott Y. H. Kim et al., *Current State of Research on Decision-making Competency of Cognitively Impaired Elderly Persons*, 10 Am. J. Geriatric Psychiatry 151 (2002).

[98] Barry Reisberg, *Senile Dementia*, in II Encyclopedia of Aging 907 915 (G. Maddox et al., eds., 2001).

[99] U.S. Department Veterans Affairs, Assessment of Competency and Capacity of the Older Adult: A Practice Guideline for Psychologists 29 (1997).

[100] Model Rules of Prof'l Conduct r. 1.14 cmt. 5 (Am. Bar Ass'n 2015).